Iron Golem

Steve the Noob

Copyright © 2015 by Steve the Noob. All rights reserved.
No part of this book may be duplicated, redistributed, or given away without prior consent from the author.

Disclaimer: This book is a work of fanfiction; it is not an official Minecraft book. It is not endorsed, authorized, licensed, sponsored, or supported by Mojang AB, Microsoft Corp. or any other entity owning or controlling rights to the Minecraft name, trademarks or copyrights.
Minecraft ®/TM & © 2009-2015 Mojang / Notch / Microsoft

All names, places, characters and all other aspects of the game mentioned from here on are trademarked and owned by their respective owners. Any other trademarks or company names mentioned in this book are the property of their respective owners and are only mentioned for identification purposes.

Thank You

Thank you for picking up a copy of my book. I spent many hours putting this book together, so I hope that you will enjoy reading it. As a Minecraft player, it brings me great joy to be able to share my stories with you. The game is fun and entertaining, and surprisingly, writing about it can be almost just as fun. Once you are done reading this book, if you enjoyed it, please take a moment to leave a review. It will help other people discover this book. If after reading it, you realize that you hate it with such passion, please feel free to leave me a review anyway. I enjoy reading what people think about my books and writing style. I hope that many people will like this book and encourage me to keep writing. Thanks in advance.

Special thanks to readers of my previous books. Thank you for taking the time to leave a review. I appreciate it so much; your support means so much to me. I will continue to keep writing and will try to provide the highest quality of unofficial Minecraft books. Thank you for your support.

Check Out My Author Page

Steve the Noob

My Other Books

Diary of Steve the Noob

Diary of Steve the Noob 2

Diary of a Minecraft Centaur

Diary of an Adventurous Steve

Diary of a Not-So-Wicked Witch

Diary of a Cowardly Chicken

Entry 1

This just might be the best idea I've ever had, and I've never had much of great ideas. If only I'd thought of this sooner. Then maybe my life would be a whole lot better right now. I would probably be loved and adored by the whole village. This will be *amazing*.

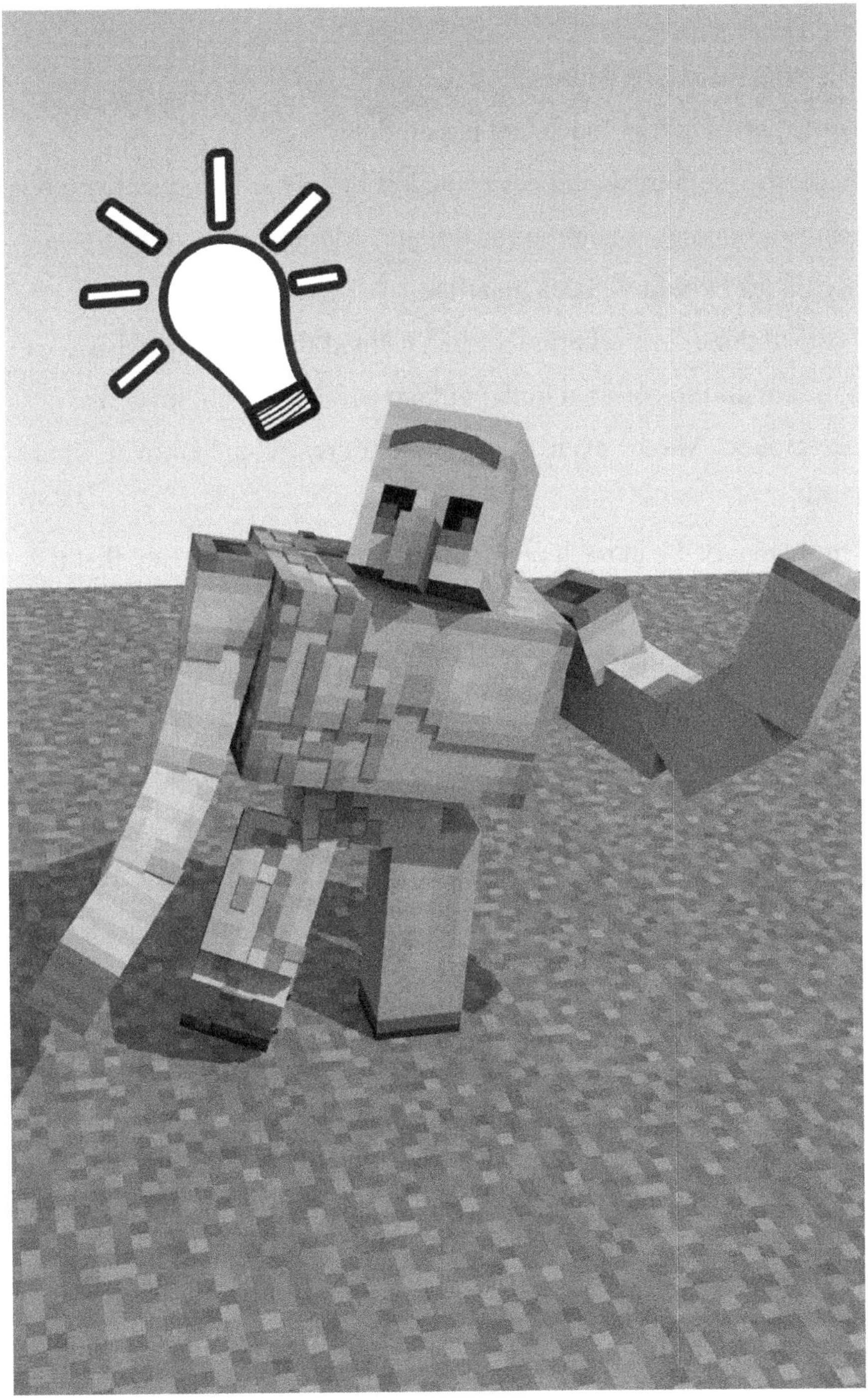

I'm pretty sure everyone will love this.

Oh, you are *such* a genius, Ryder.

Now, just one final touch and it's all done.

I take the paintbrush and cover the last bit of the swing-set with blue paint. Who knew I could be so artistic? Maybe this could've been my thing! I could've been an artist!

"Ah, all done!" I exclaim. I've just painted the swing-set blue.

I'm sure all the children in the village will absolutely love this playground. Maybe even all the non-children would enjoy it. I know I will.

Hmm, maybe I can try it out. You know, just to make sure that it's working—not 'coz I really want to ride the swing.

Yep, here I go. Just testing out the swing set.

"Wow, this is *really* fun!" I say to myself since there is no one around to talk to.

Who knew?! It's really been quite a while since I've been on a swing set—not since I fell off one when I was still little. Of course, it didn't do that much damage to me since I *am* made of iron. But the kid I crashed into wasn't as sturdy as me.

That was just an unfortunate accident, of course. I mean, it's not like I fell off the swing on purpose! What did I know? I was just a kid! But really, the kids of the village need to have more fun! I really can't understand why they wouldn't build a playground in the village. Those kids are missing out!

Now I know that this really *is* a genius idea! All the kids in the village will surely love me!

"Oh, I just can't wait to show this to everyone!"

Maybe I should go and prepare now.

Whoops. Wait a minute. I think my butt is stuck.

I stand from the swing slowly. It feels pretty hard—like I said, my butt seems stuck. But I pull up my back-end from the swing. I feel it slowly detaching.

I finally stand straight on my feet.

"Ugh, what is on my butt?!" I say. It really does feel sticky!

I reach behind to see what I might've sat on. I look at my fingers.

Uh-oh. My fingers are *blue*!

I turn around and look at the swing.

Oh, no. There in the middle of the swing seat is a butt-shaped bare spot without paint on it. And the paint that should be there is on my butt.

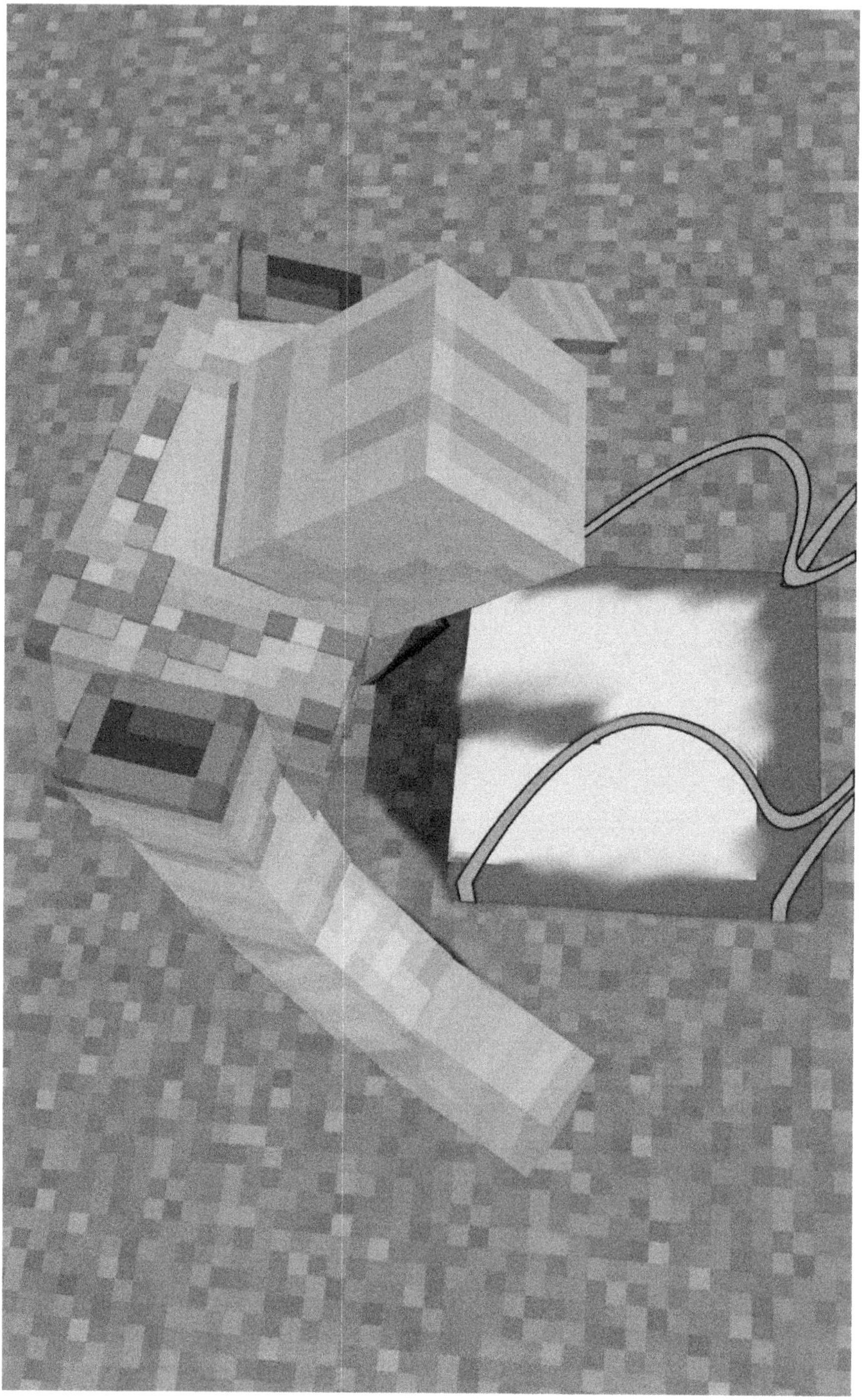

Great. That is just absolutely great! I sat on wet paint and destroyed my butt *and* the swing set. They really should put labels on these like 'wet paint' to warn people.

No, wait. *I* made this.

Yes, I am quite the genius.

But wait. I think I can still fix this! I can just paint over the spot that I sat on! Oh, I really *am* a genius!

"Now, where is that can of paint?" I ask myself.

I walk over to the large can of blue paint beside the monkey bars. I peer inside.

It's empty! I must've used up all of it on the swing set. It *is* quite a big swing set.

But now what am I supposed to do?! Where am I going to get paint for the swing set?

Maybe I can get some paint from the other stuff here! I'm pretty sure I put on a bit of excess paint on the slide.

I take the paint brush from the can and run back to the slide. I brush off some of the paint from the slide. Some blue paint sticks to the brush.

"Hah! I think this could work!"

I run back to the swing and try to put the blue paint on it.

"Wait, I don't think this could work," I say as I inspect the brush.

The paint has dried up! Now I wouldn't be able to paint on the swing set.

Oh! I know! Maybe I can get some of the paint on my butt back to the seat! I think it's still pretty wet.

I sit back down on the swing set and try to press the paint back onto the seat. I wiggle my butt, trying to get as much paint off as possible. I do that for a few minutes.

"Ryder?" I hear someone call out.

Someone's there! This really isn't the best moment for someone to see me. Ugh! This will be absolutely humiliating! Maybe if I pretend not to hear him, he'll go away.

I freeze on the seat.

"Ryder? Is that you?" the voice says again. Now, he sounds closer, like he's just right behind me.

I groan. I guess he won't be going away soon.

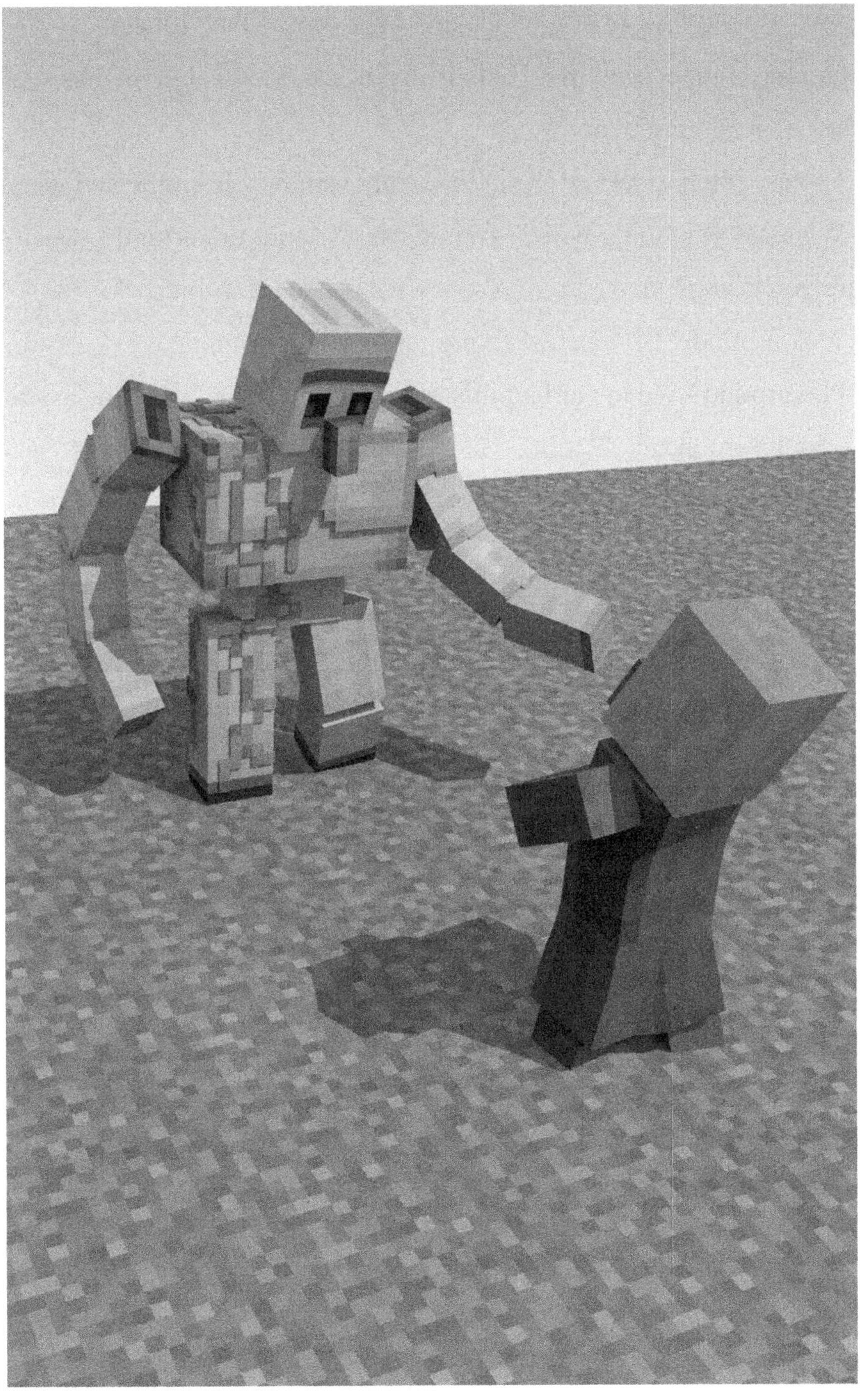

I turn around towards the voice and I see one of the villagers standing right behind me. He is frowning, and looks like he has seen the craziest thing ever.

"Y-Yes. Oh, hi, Gerald!" I say, casually standing from the swing set.

"What are you doing here?" Gerald asks. "More importantly, what are you *doing*?"

I look around. "I-I was just fixing up this playground."

"Playground? We never had this playground before," Gerald says as he looks around.

"Well, yeah. I built it," I say.

Gerald looks at me with wide eyes. I don't understand, but he looks kind of terrified. I don't think I look that scary. Unless there's actually a ghost floating behind me.

I quickly turn around.

Hmm, looks like I'm still alone—except for Gerald, of course.

"*You* built this? Are you sure?" Gerald says. "I mean, are you sure it won't go crumbling down? Or it won't go collapsing on all the children?"

"No, of course not! I already tried it out!" I say.

"But why is your butt blue?"

"Huh?"

"Your butt. It is blue," Gerald points out.

I twist to look at my butt. "Oh, yeah. I kind of sat on the swing with wet paint."

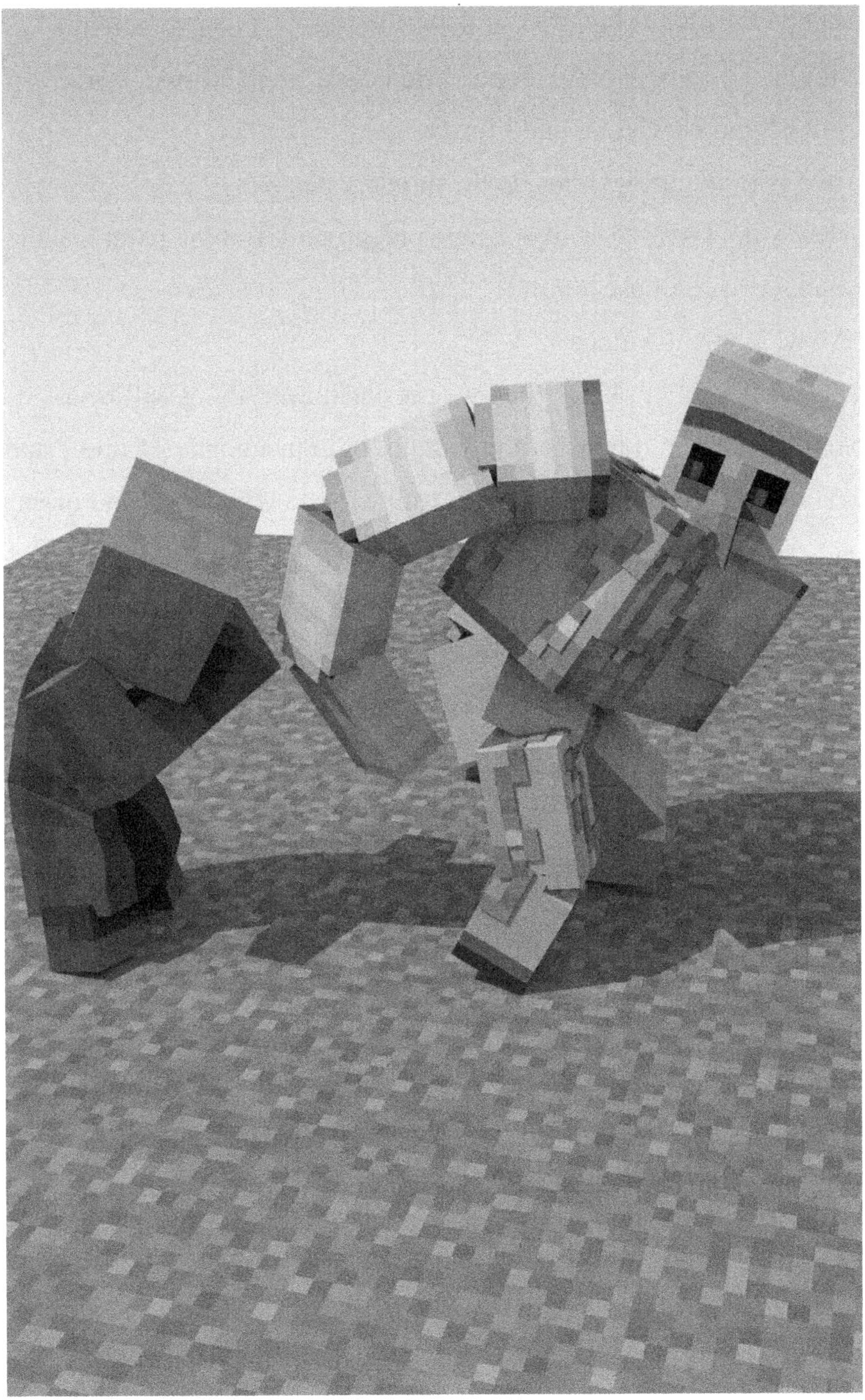

Gerald chuckles as he looks at the swing set. "Of course you did."
"Hey! Is this a new playground?" we hear a smaller, tinier voice from behind us. Gerald and I turn around.
A kid is standing right beside the monkey bars.
"Hey, kid," I say. "Yes, it *is* a new playground. But the paint is still wet, so you can't use it yet."
"Aww!" the kid whines.
"Just wait for a bit, kid. When we get back, everything will be a-okay!" I tell him. I then turn to Gerald. "I'm just gonna go home and get cleaned up. Wouldn't want to walk around with blue paint on my butt. Wanna come with me?"
"Actually, I think I'll just stay here and, uh, you know… watch the playground while you're gone," Gerald says as he takes his position beside the entrance I made. "You know? Just to make sure that…" he closes the iron gate I created, "no one gets hurt."
"Oh, yeah, of course," I say. "Should've thought of that. Thanks, Gerald! I'll be right back in a jiffy."
I run back to the house to clean myself up.
I am so excited to see the look on everyone's faces once they see the playground! Oh, I hope lots of people will get to see it today.
I should probably go back now. Wouldn't want to miss the villagers' reactions!
"Playground, here I come!" I say as I lock the door and slam the door shut.
I take a few steps out and realized something.
"Wait. I think I left my keys."
I walk back to the door and try the knob. Yep, it's locked alright.

"Great! I must've forgotten them inside," I say to myself. "Ugh. I guess I'm gonna have to break the door down to get my keys."

I take a few steps away from the door. I position myself, and then I hurl myself right at the door, making it collapse into my house.

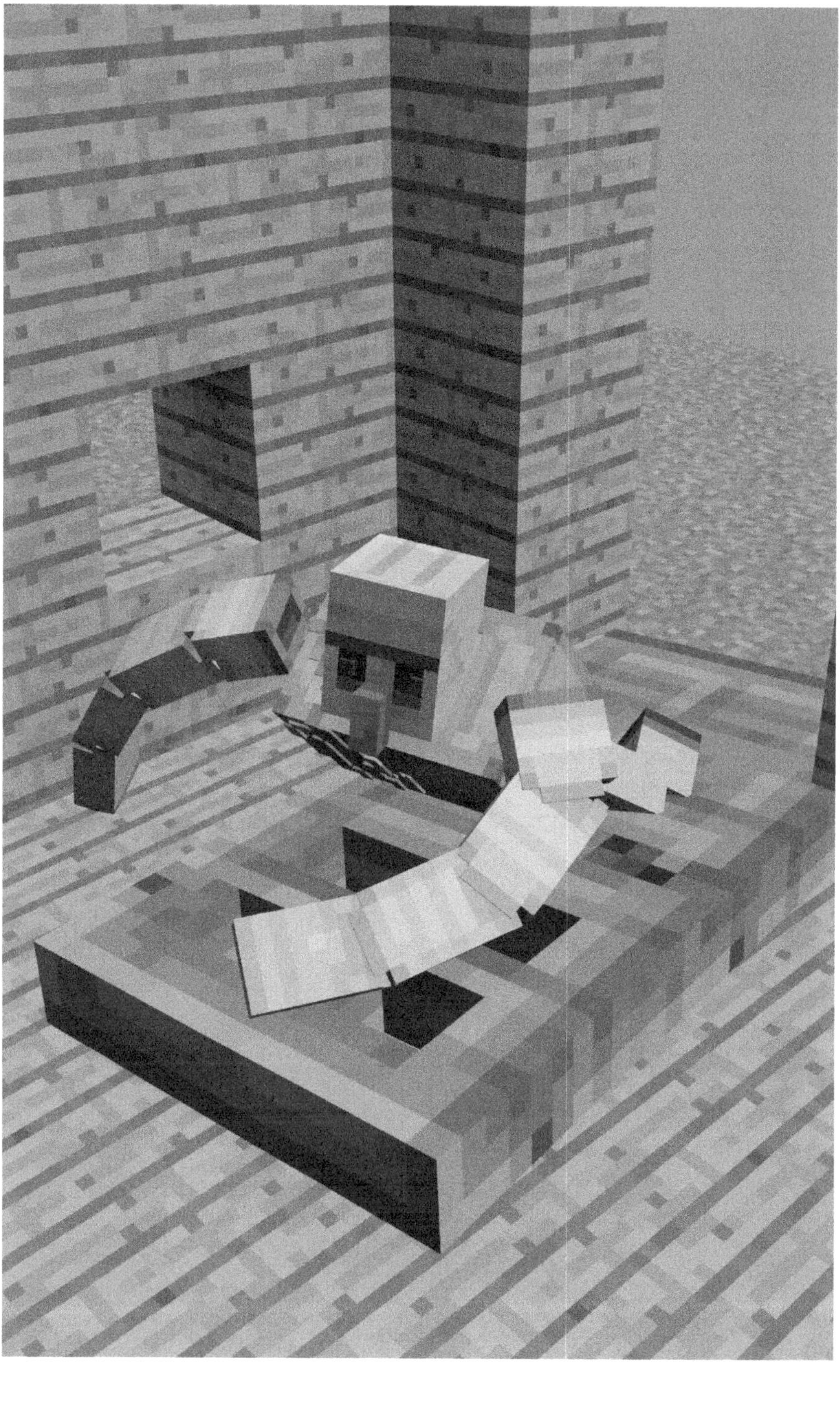

"Well, that was pretty easy," I say as I walk to my bed and looked for my keys.

See, these are the times that I am absolutely grateful that I am an iron golem. Breaking things down with my body isn't that much of a burden.

I grab the keys from the table and walk back out the door. I reach for the door knob—which I can't seem to find.

"Oh, right," I say as I look at the blank space where the door should be. "Well, I guess I just gotta hope that no one steals anything from the house."

I run back to the playground and see quite possibly all of the villagers' kids hanging out by the entrance. I walk up to Gerald, who is still standing guard at the entrance.

"Gerald, what's with all these kids?" I ask.

"They all wanted to come in, but I didn't want to let them in without your permission," Gerald says.

I turn to look at the kids. They all look absolutely excited to play. It's exactly how I imagined they would be.

I turn back to Gerald with a wide grin on my face. "Sure, go right ahead," I say.

I walk to the slide and start picking up some metallic junk on the ground. "Wait! I should probably keep this now. Wouldn't want the kids to trip on these!"

"Are those nuts and bolts?!" Gerald says as I pick up the little metal thingies on the grass.

"Uh, I think so?" I say. I'm really not so sure what these things do.

"Where did you get those?!" he exclaims as he grabs the metal stuff from my hands.

"I... Uh, it was with the swing set... and the slide... and the seesaw," I answer.

"Well, what were they doing on the ground?!"

"I didn't think they were important," I say. "Plus, I wasn't sure where to put them."

"Not important?!" Gerald exclaims. "These hold those things together! Without these, the whole playground will--"

Suddenly, we hear a loud creaking. It sounds like metals grinding together.

Gerald and I turn to the playground. It seems like the swing set is leaning forward. So are the slide and the seesaw.

It continues to lean forward—dangerously forward. The whole playground is leaning closer to the ground until...

Everything collapses to the ground.

The whole playground shatters and breaks apart. Metal pipes, metal sheets, swing seats, ropes, and chains scatter around the ground. The playground is destroyed.

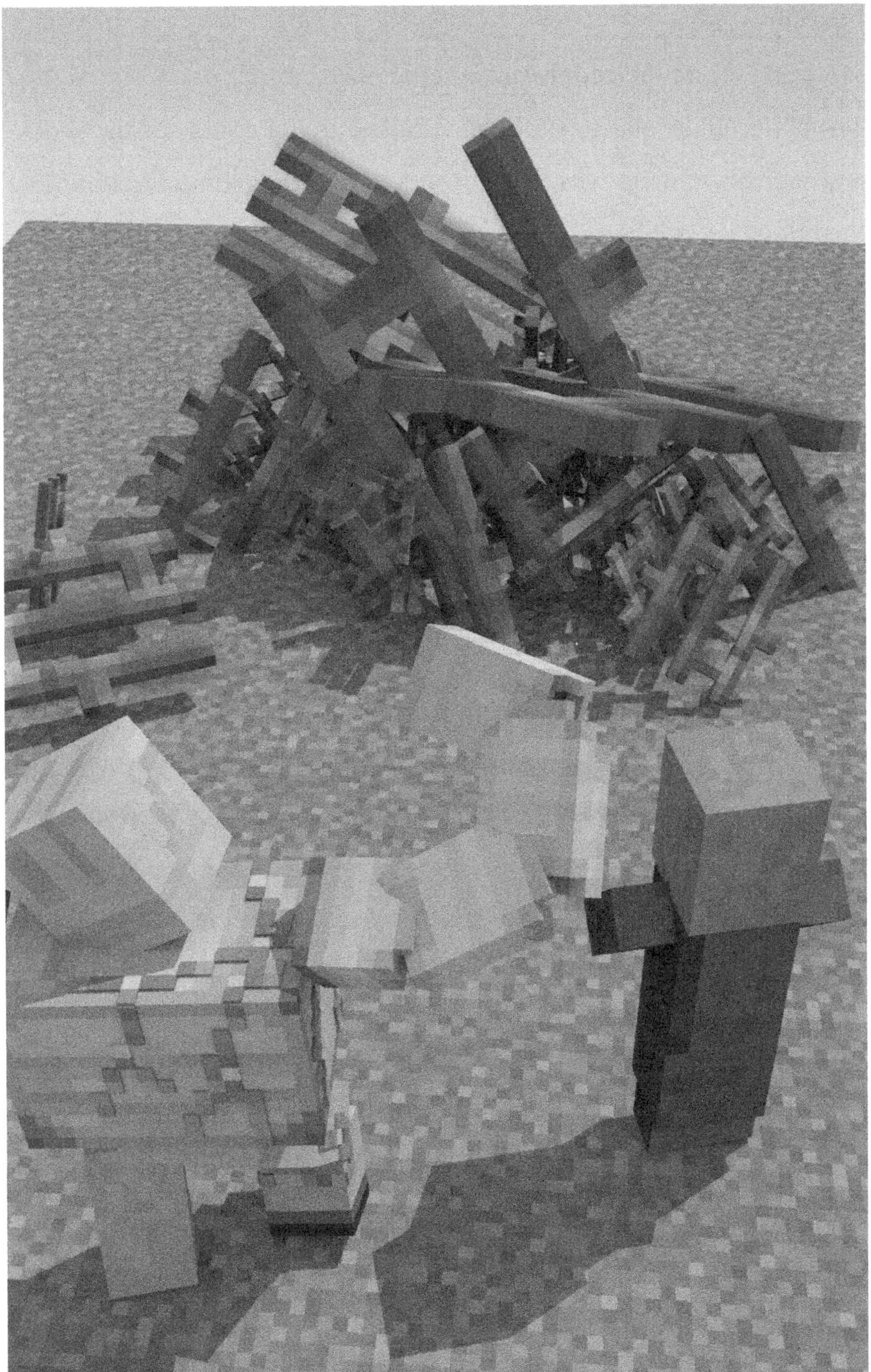

Everyone gasps.

I turn to look at the people outside the playground.

The children are staring at the devastated area. I could see the shock and sadness in their eyes. It's absolutely heartbreaking. Every one of them looks at me like I've just shattered their hopes and dreams—which, in a way, I kind of did.

"Great job, Ryder!" I hear someone sarcastically say from the crowd.

"Yeah, nice job putting it together, Ryder," comes another snide comment.

"What a doof," says another.

I turn and see the crowd slowly leaving one by one. They all leave until the only ones left are a few children still looking expectantly but sadly at the playground.

"We really wanted to play in there," says one of them before they all walk away.

I turn back to the playground and look around at the broken stuff that I just made.

"At least you're lucky that no one else was trying 'em out! You could've caused another accident!" Gerald exclaims.

I nod. "You're right. That would've been bad," I say.

"Did you even tried them out?!" Gerald asks.

"I did! I mean, I did sit on the swing set a while ago. I'm not sure why it wasn't destroyed when I did," I tell him.

"Well, maybe it didn't because you're such an airhead!" he exclaims.

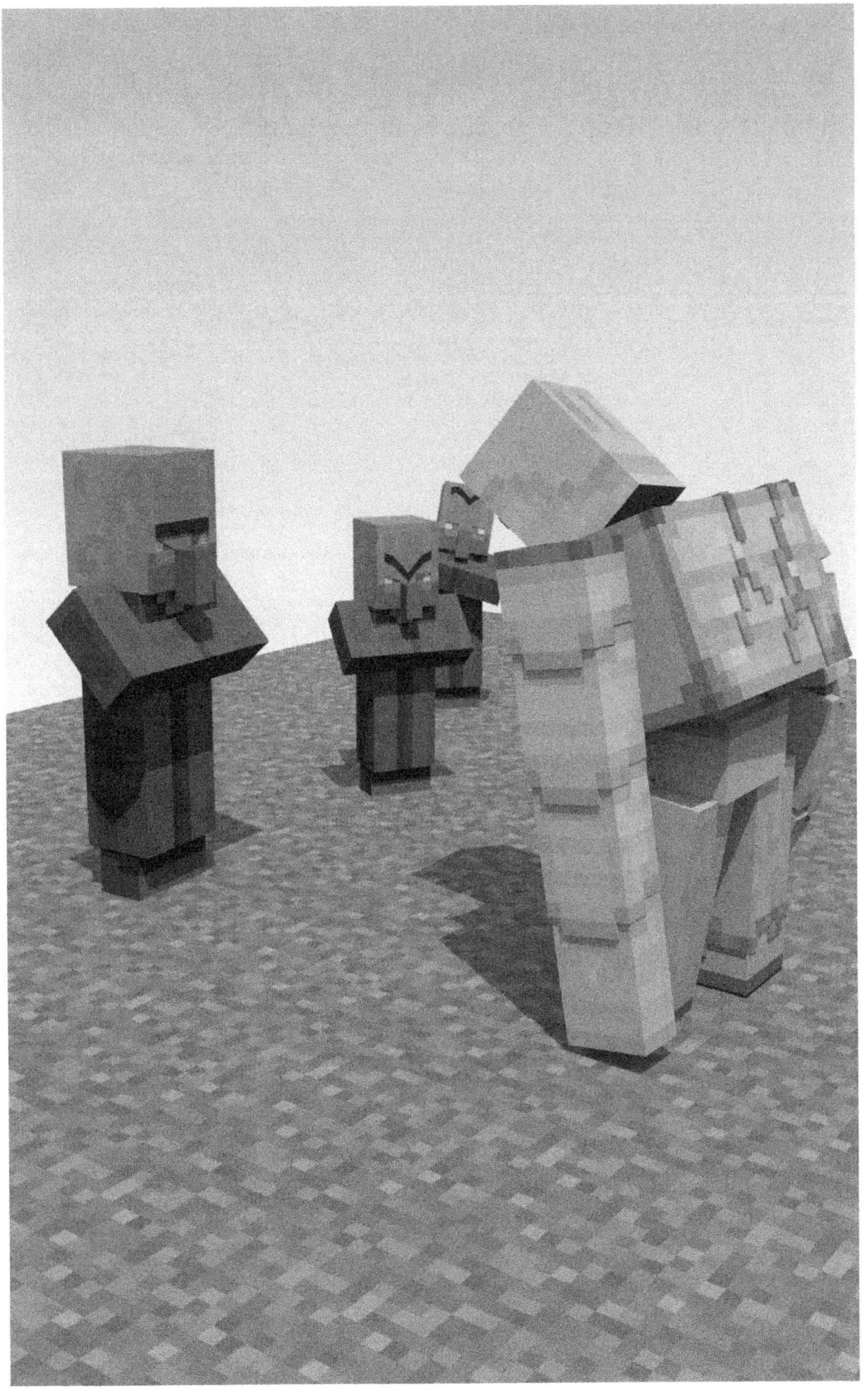

I sigh as I continue to walk around.

"But at least no one got in an accident!" I say again. "But that *was* a complete waste of time. I wish it would've worked."

Entry 2

What a wonderful morning! This is truly a great morning. The sun is shining brightly through the space where my door should've been. Yup, everyone's looking into my house. But hey, at least it's bright inside.

I believe that this really is going to be an amazing day. I can feel it! I feel like I'm going to do something amazingly great today.

But first, breakfast.

Uh-oh. I'm all out of milk. Great. Now what am I supposed to put in my cereal?

Hmm. I have coffee, orange juice, macaroni soup… Oh, that soup is white like milk. Maybe I can put *that* in my cereal.

I pour some of the soup into the bowl filled with cereal.

Now, for a taste.

Oh, wow. Bleh. That is *terrible*! It doesn't even taste edible! I think that soup just turned sour. Ugh. Whose idea was this?!

Wait, it's mine.

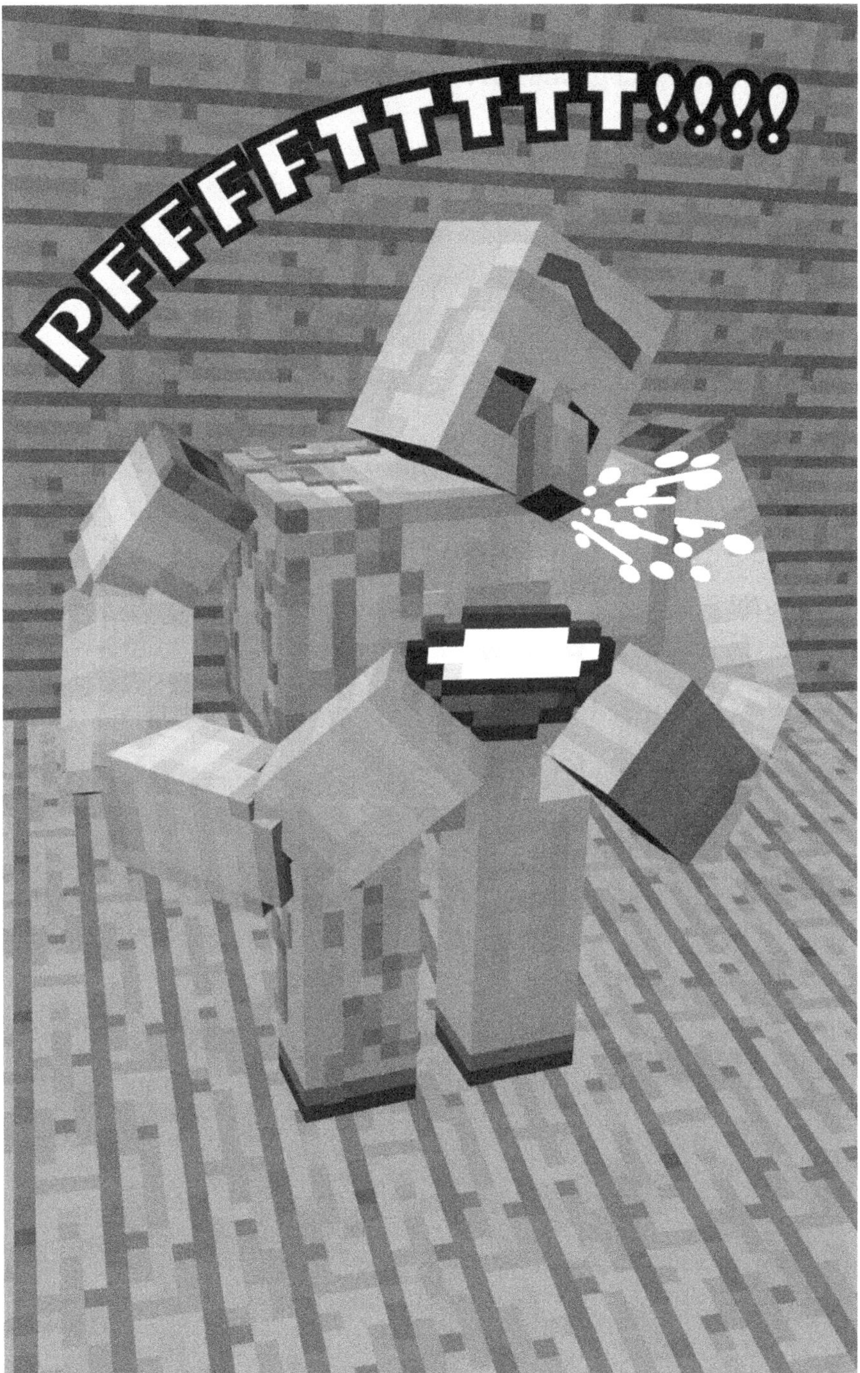
PFFFFTTTTTT!!!!

Well, this is just not the best idea I've had. Yep, it was a terrible idea. Guess I'm just gonna have to skip breakfast now. I'm gonna starve to death.

"Hey, Ryder," I hear someone from the door. And since I don't actually have a door, all I need to do is look out.

"Oh, hey, Sam," I say. It's one of my very few neighbors.

He walks inside my house. "Where's your door?" he asks.

"It's, uh, kind of a long story. What are you doing here?"

"I was just going to ask what you're doing today," he asks. I can see him looking around the house nervously.

"Oh. I haven't really thought about it yet. Why? Is today a special occasion?" People rarely ask what I'm doing. I just usually go and make plans by myself.

"Why? Do you think there's a special occasion?" Sam asks. He looks at me and waits for my answer.

I think back and try to remember what date it is. Ugh. I'm really not good at this. Sometimes I even forget about my own birthday!

"No, I don't think so," I answer.

Suddenly, a grin appears on his lips. "Oh, alright. Great," he says. Why is he suddenly so cheery? "Well, I think you should just stay in for today, you know? Get some rest. You must be extremely tired with all the work you did. I heard you made a playground the other day."

"Yeah, but it really didn't work out."

He starts heading for the door—well, that area where the door should be. "I gotta go. But take my advice. Take the day off. I mean it!" Then Sam completely walks out of my house.

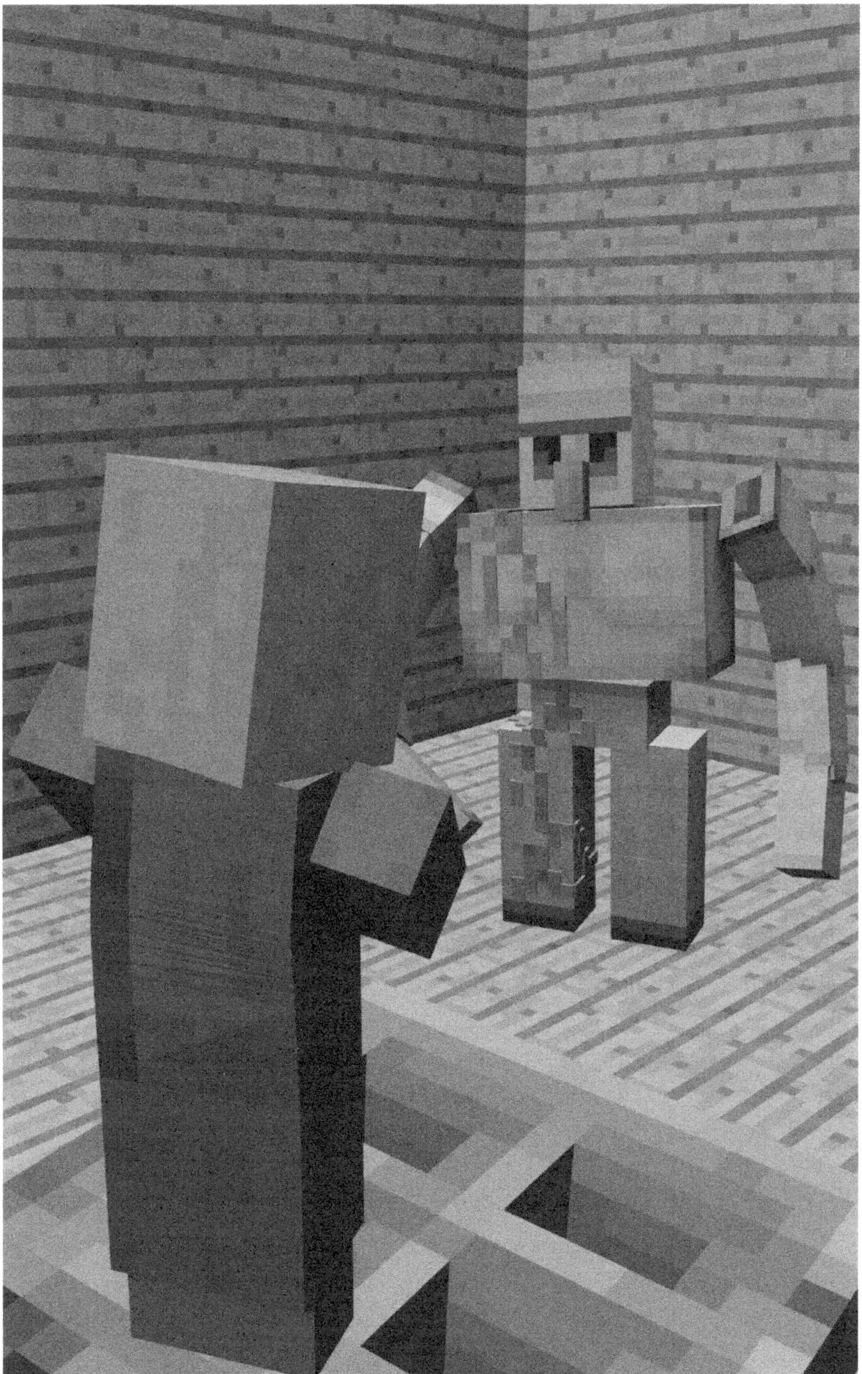

I think something's up. Or maybe not. But I do like his advice of resting for the day. Maybe I will.

Wait, why is there so many people outside?

I look out of my door. People are scurrying around. It seems like they all have some place to be. They seem pretty excited, too.

What could be going on?

I walk out. There are even children running around, and they seem all dressed-up.

"Hey, kid!" I say to one child running across the street. The kid stops in front of me. "What's going on? Where are you guys going?"

"It's the chief's birthday! They're having a party at the village square," says the kid. "They said there's going to be lots of toys and candy!" And then he runs off.

"Oh, so *that's* what's going on," I say to myself. "It's a birthday party!"

That party's gotta be big. I mean, it's the chief's party after all—he's the leader of this village. He surely deserves the best.

I should probably do something for him, too! I do, after all, have quite amazing ideas up in my sleeve.

I could bake a cake for him! But everyone else is probably making him cakes, too. I've got to think bigger.

Oh, I know! A bigger cake! Ah! You are such a genius, Ryder!

I'm going to bake the biggest cake this village has ever seen! I'm going to make it as big as my house! Yep! That's what I'm going to do.

Guess I'd have to buy some supplies.

Wait. I don't know how to bake. I can't even bake a small cupcake! How am I supposed to bake a gigantic birthday cake now?! I can't give the chief some lame uncooked cake! I'd have to think of some other thing to give him as a surprise.

Oh, I know! His birthday should be celebrated with a big *bang*! I shall fix up a firework display at his party. It will be absolutely marvelous! I should go now and buy all the fireworks I can get before anyone else buys first.

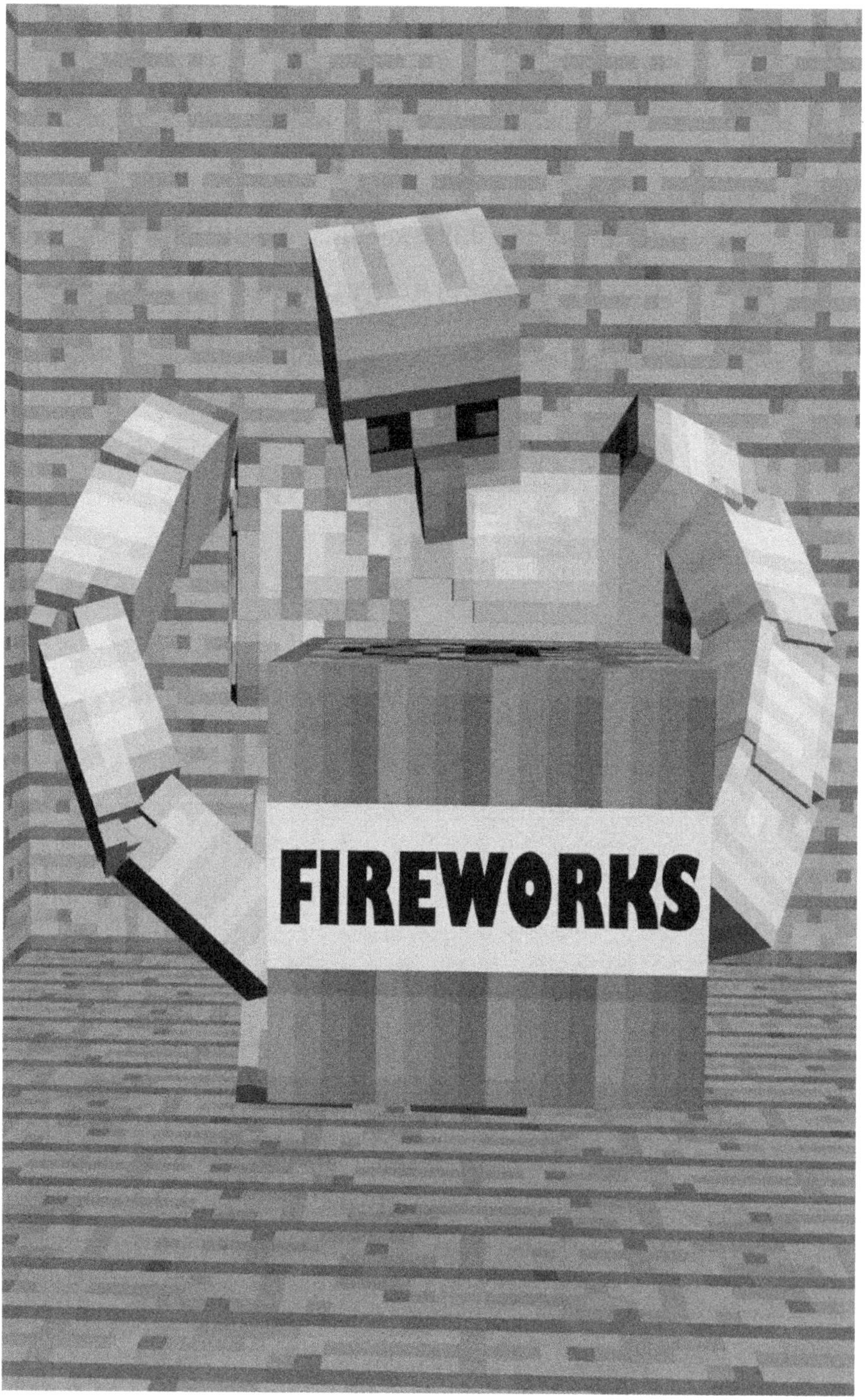
FIREWORKS

I'll just take one more sip from my soup/cereal—

Ugh. Bleh. I never learn.

I run out of my house and go straight to the shop.

The streets in the outskirts of town are already quite empty. I'm pretty sure everyone's already at the village square, celebrating with the chief. That means that everyone will be able to see my awesome surprise.

I take the huge boxes to my position.

By the way, I was right—everyone really is already at the village square. The place is filled with villagers eating, drinking, laughing, and even children running around and playing.

Since everyone is too preoccupied with celebrating, no one could see me run to the back of the village hall—this is where the chief's office is. But that's not where I'm supposed to go.

I tiptoe inside and search for the stairs.

"Aha!" I exclaim when I see the staircase. Oh, wait, I really shouldn't be talking too loud if I'm snooping around without permission. I put a hand over my mouth.

And then the huge box of fireworks in my arms toppled to the ground.

I kneel down on the ground as I chase around the fireworks rolling all around. I pick 'em all up and put them back in the box. When I've gotten all the explosives around me, I take the box into my arms.

Huh. It seems to weigh a bit lighter. Oh, well, maybe the fireworks lost weight from all that rolling around.

I tiptoe up the stairs to continue my mission. No one's around. Everyone is outside celebrating with the chief.

I climb up onto the rooftop. It's a wide clear space, perfect to set up my firework display. There are just some wooden chairs and craters gathered in the corner. Hmm, that could be a good place to set up.

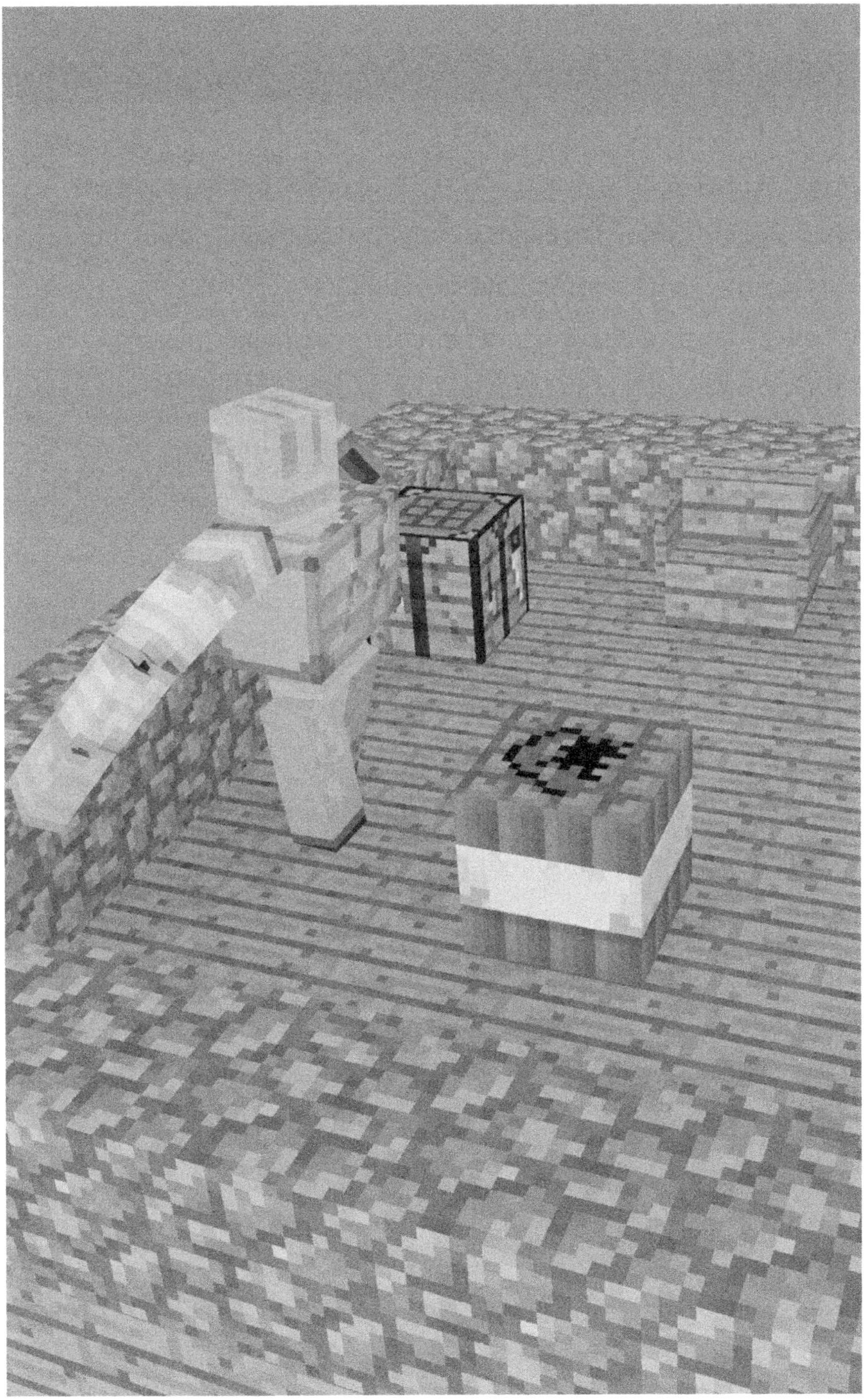

I start to take out the fireworks out of the box. I also brought candles so that I can light up the fireworks much easily. Maybe I should light the candles first.

After taking out all of the fireworks in the box, I bring out the candles, too. I make the candles stand on the rooftop. And then, I light them up with my flint and steel tool.

Whew, it's a good thing that it isn't that windy today.

I keep the flames burning and then go on to put up the fireworks. How do I do this? Oh, so the fireworks come with a tiny rope at the end of it. Maybe I should tie them all together! Or even at least tie them up by threes.

So I gather up all the fireworks and start tying them together with those tiny ropes at the bottom. I'm pretty sure this would be absolutely beautiful in the skies.

Wow, it smells like someone's been cooking.

No, wait, it smells like someone's *trying* to cook, but it's already burning. Something's burning!

I turn around.

The wooden crates and chairs are burning! The flames are consuming them all up! Dark smoke rises as the flames continue to grow.

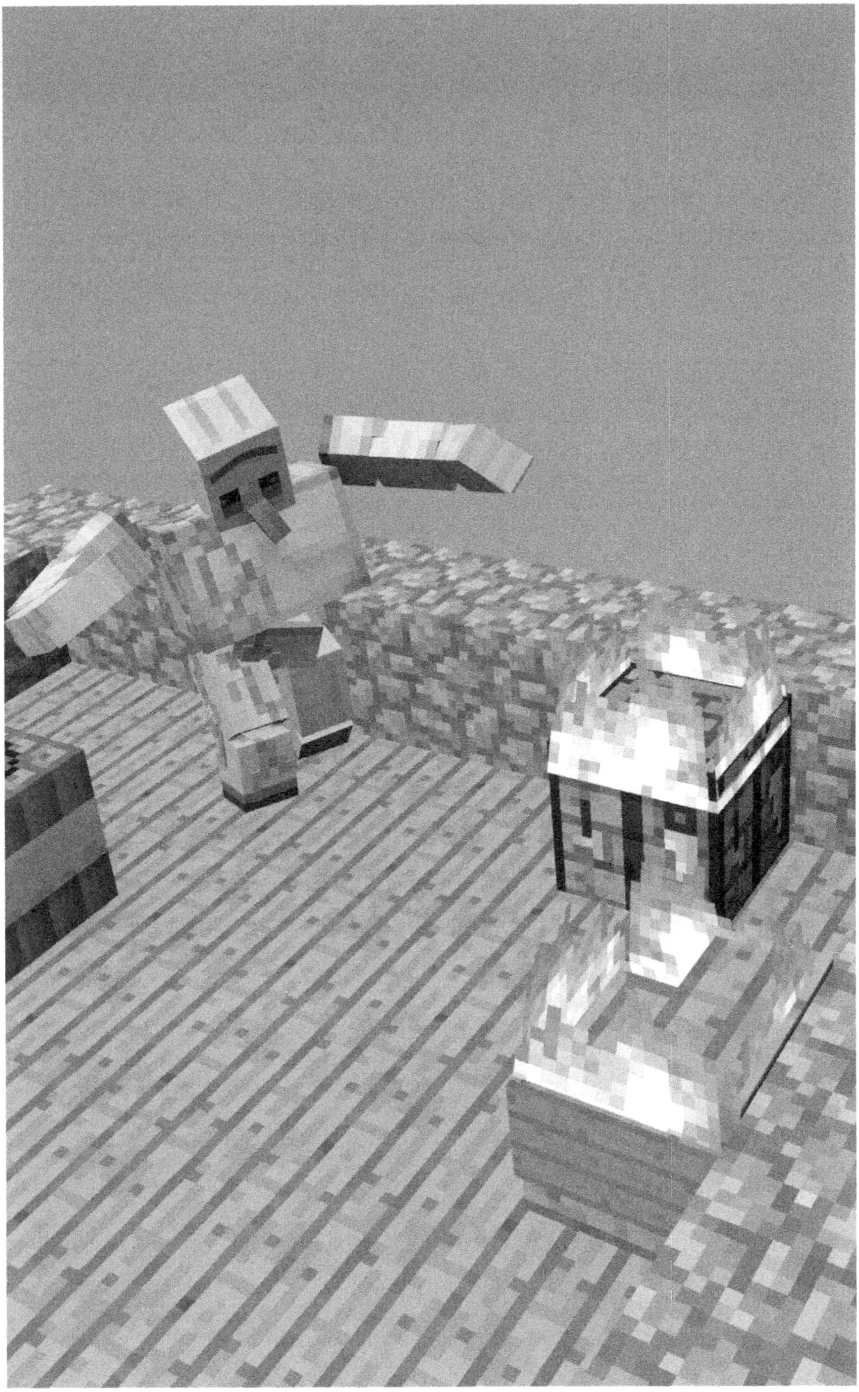

Near the flames are the candles I put up, but they had all toppled over to the floor.

I look around for water—or anything that could possibly put out the fire. I see a blanket draped over the rails of the rooftop. I think I've read something before about putting a blanket over the flames.

I cover the fire completely with the blanket. The flames disappear under it.

"I did it!" I exclaim.

Whoosh.

The flames appear again. And this time, it's getting bigger.

"Whoa! What do I do?!" I say even though there's no one around to hear me.

I take a step back. The fire is spreading towards the tied up fireworks on the floor. It's spreading like—well, like fire.

BOOM! BOOM! BOOM!

Three fireworks just exploded. It shot straight up to the skies.

I hear people gasp from below.

"Look! There's a fire on the rooftop!" I hear someone else yell from the villagers.

BOOM! BOOM! BOOM!

Three more fireworks rocket up into the sky. I could hear screams coming from the villagers. I peer over the rails, and I could see them all running around.

Now that I think of it, I don't think I should be up here. I should probably get down there and run with the villagers. Yeah, I think it's safer down there.

I run back to the stairs, down the building, and out into the village square.

Everyone's still running around, trying to find cover. But I'm pretty sure it's really a lot safer down here. I mean, the fireworks would be far away from me.

But then again, I spoke too soon.

From the rooftop, I see what seems like a fireball flying towards me. That does not look good.

I dive into a crater beside me just as the fireball whooshes just inches away from my face. It hits the fruit stand behind me. The stand exploded!

More screams.

More fireworks.

More explosions.

But no more village hall.

After what seems like countless hours of screaming, running, and chaos, everything is finally calm. Well, it *sounds* calm.

The fire has been extinguished. My fireworks are all out. And the screaming has ended.

The village square is in shambles. Booths and stalls have been destroyed. The village hall is devastated.

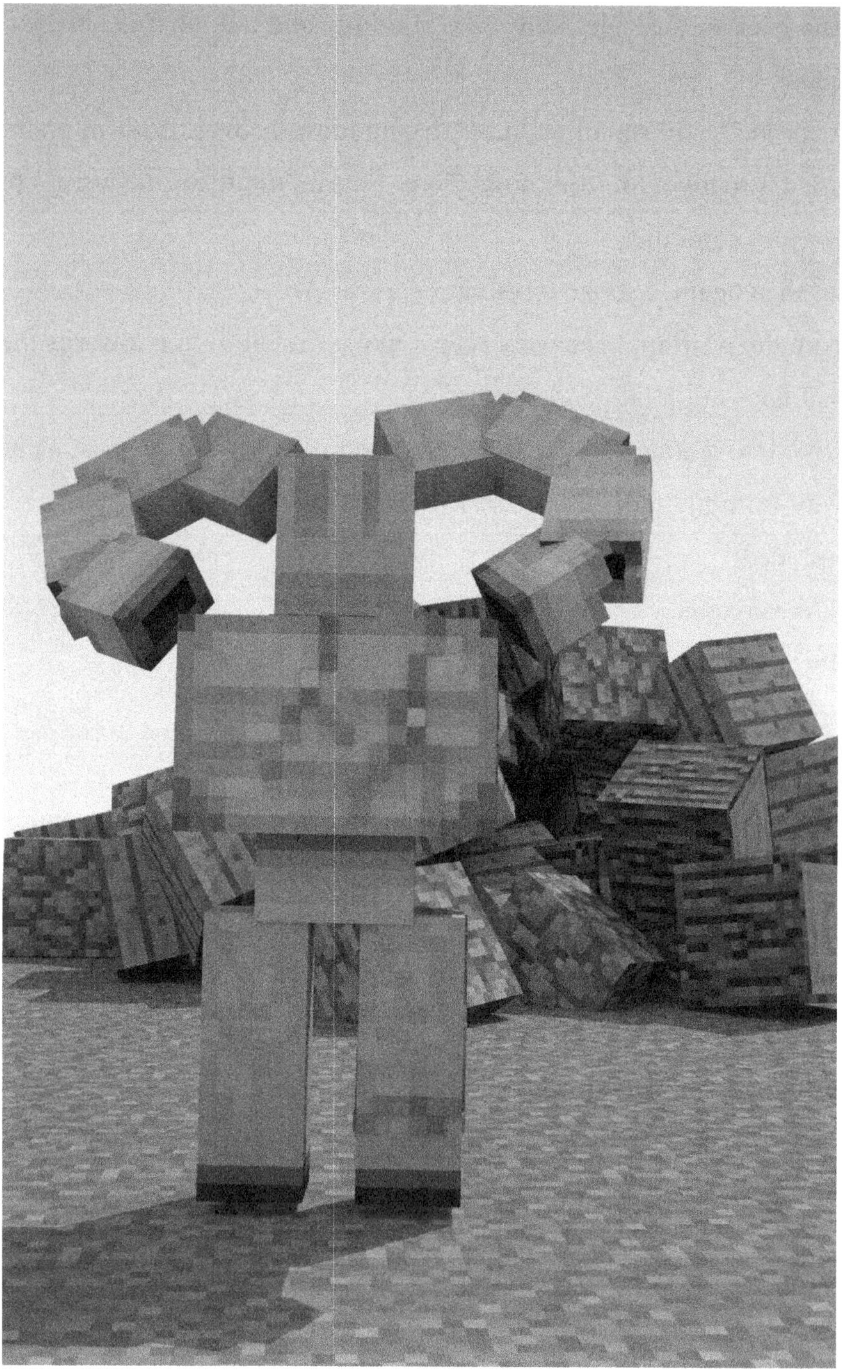

"What happened?" says the chief as he looks at the aftermath. He's standing just a few meters away from me.

The guards come up to the chief and show him some black burnt box thing. "We might know who caused this, sir."

The chief looks at the burnt box thing and reads it, "Property of Ryder."

Everyone's head turns to me and glares.

Gulp.

An officer grabs my arm and shoves me forward.

"Ow! You're hurting me!" I exclaim. The officer pulls me towards the center of the village square. I could feel all eyes on me.

We stop in front of the chief.

"Ryder," he says with so much authority. I already feel so ashamed just hearing his low and deep voice.

I keep my head down. "Y-Yes, sir."

"Look at me," he says.

So I look up.

He holds up the black scrap in his hand. "What is the meaning of this?"

"U-Uh," I stutter.

"Why is your name written here?" Chief asks.

"I didn't want anyone to touch my stuff," I answer.

"So this *is* yours?" another office butts in.

"Well, yeah," I say.

Everyone gasps.

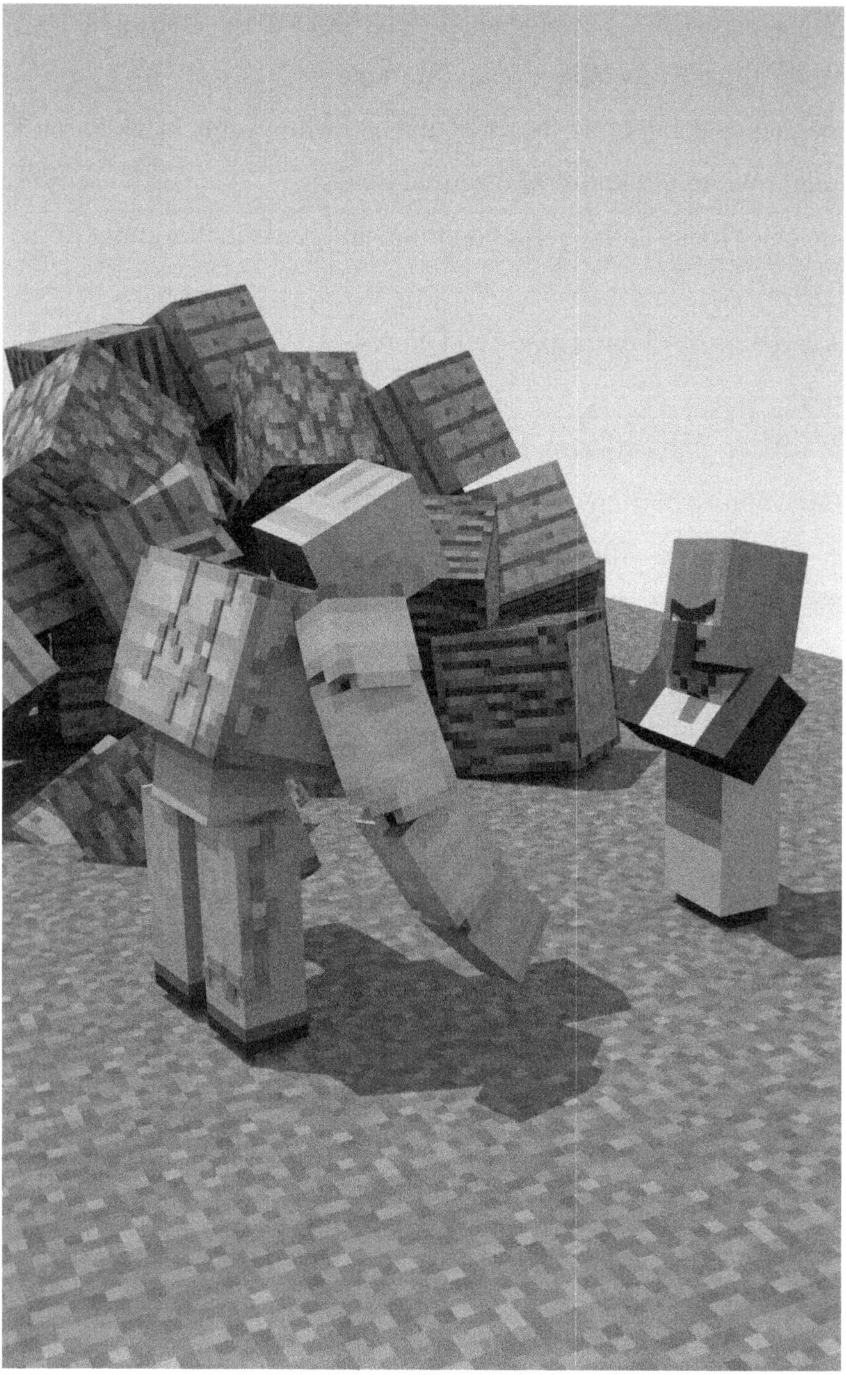

"You caused those explosions?" the chief asks with eyes wide in disbelief. "What did you *do*? What *were* those?"

"Fireworks," I answer. "I bought lots of fireworks."

"Why?!" asks someone from the villagers.

"It's the chief's birthday!" I tell them with a grin. "It's a surprise."

"What?!" says the chief.

I turn to him and smile. This is kind of a big deal for me—talking to the Chief. I didn't even know that he knew who I was!

"It was a birthday surprise for you, Chief," I say. "Happy birthday!"

Silence.

Chief is looking at me with wide eyes. His jaw drops. Everybody else is doing the same thing. They must be pretty surprised at what I did. Maybe they're even amazed! I mean, who else could think of such an amazing thing like this?

"What were you *thinking*?!" Chief suddenly exclaims, breaking the silence.

Then everyone else starts to talk all at once.

"Look at what you've done!" I hear someone say.

"Have you lost your mind?!" someone else yells.

"You could've thought about this!" exclaims another.

"What an idiot!"

Oh, wow. Ouch. I never knew words could hurt so much. Nobody has called me an idiot before. Well, maybe someone has. But I didn't think they meant it. But now, I can hear how much he—or she—meant it.

"Look at what you did!" says a villager.

I look around. Everyone's glaring at me. They are all wagging their fingers at me. Everyone looks so angry. I've never seen the villagers this angry before.

"You destroyed the village square! Everything's ruined!" I hear another say.

Smoke is still rising from the burnt village hall. The stalls and food booths—well, what's left of them, anyway—are scattered on the ground. Some parts are burned, some have turned as black as charcoal. There are still some flames scattered around.

But they're right. Everything *is* ruined.

"What do you have to say for yourself, Ryder?!" the chief asks.

"I'm…sorry?" I say. I'm not really sure what to say.

What I'm sure of is that I *did* destroy a lot of things. And that pretty much everyone's pissed at me. I've never had this many people hate me before.

It doesn't feel good.

"You should be!" yells someone from the crowd.

Angry yells and scolding comes roaring from the crowd yet again.

"What are we going to do about the village square now? *And* the village hall?" the chief asks. He looks at me, and then looks at the villagers.

"Oh, I can help! I can help fix everything!" I volunteer.

Suddenly, loud and angry talking erupts from the villagers. I don't think they like my idea very much. Everyone's retaliating.

"I think you've done enough, Ryder," says the Chief. "Just go home. We can handle this without you."

The villagers cheer and agree with the chief.

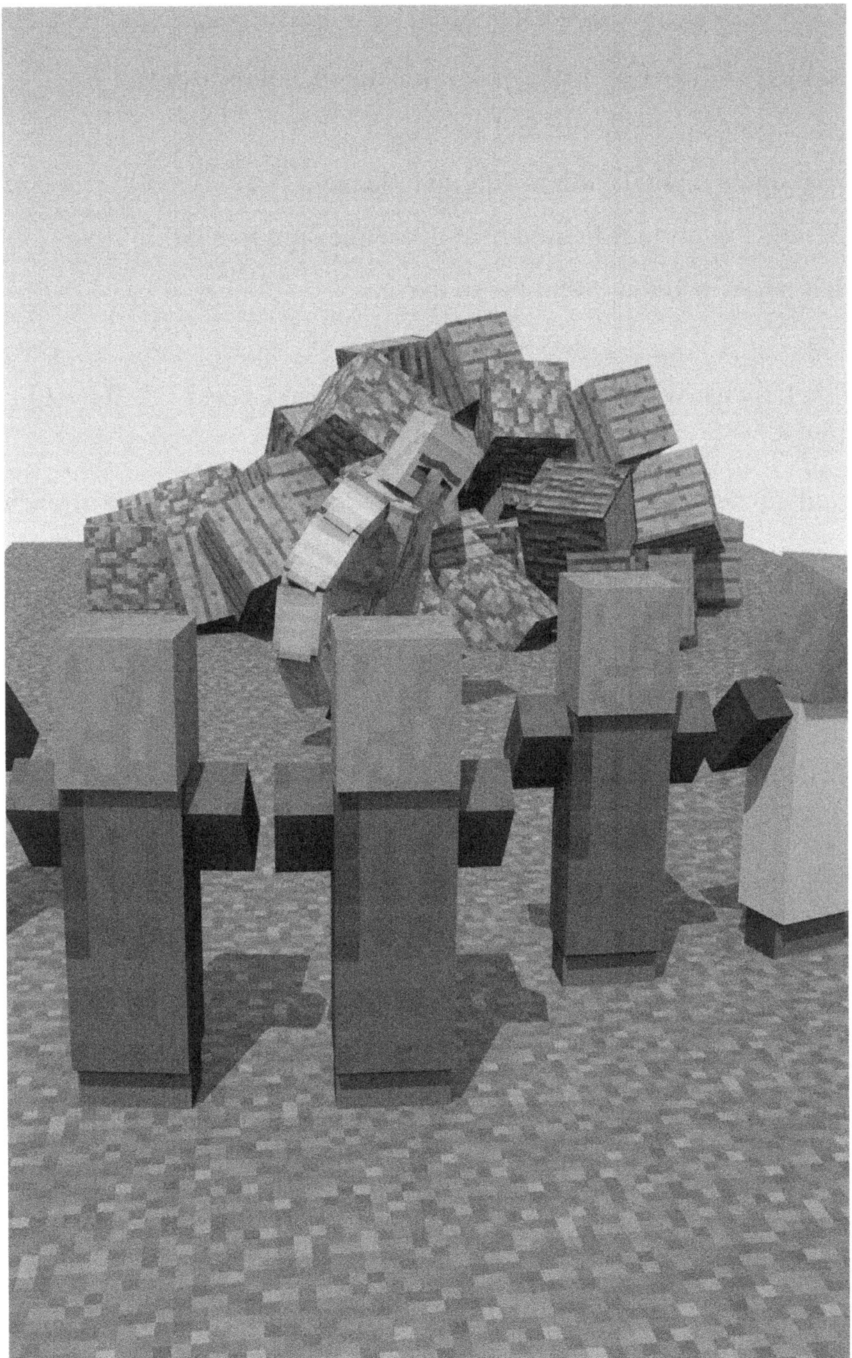

Wow. They really don't want me to be involved in any way. I can see their enthusiasm. Funny how this much enthusiasm and excitement can make me feel so bad.

Everyone's really trying to get me to leave.

"Alright," I answer. I could hear everyone sigh in relief.

That's how bad they want me to leave.

Sigh.

If that's what will make everyone happy, then I guess I do have to leave.

I walk away from the middle of the crowd. The villagers are already starting to mind their own business and are trying to fix up the mess around. I would help, but nobody wants it.

I go back to my door-less house. I lie on my bed and stare at the ceiling.

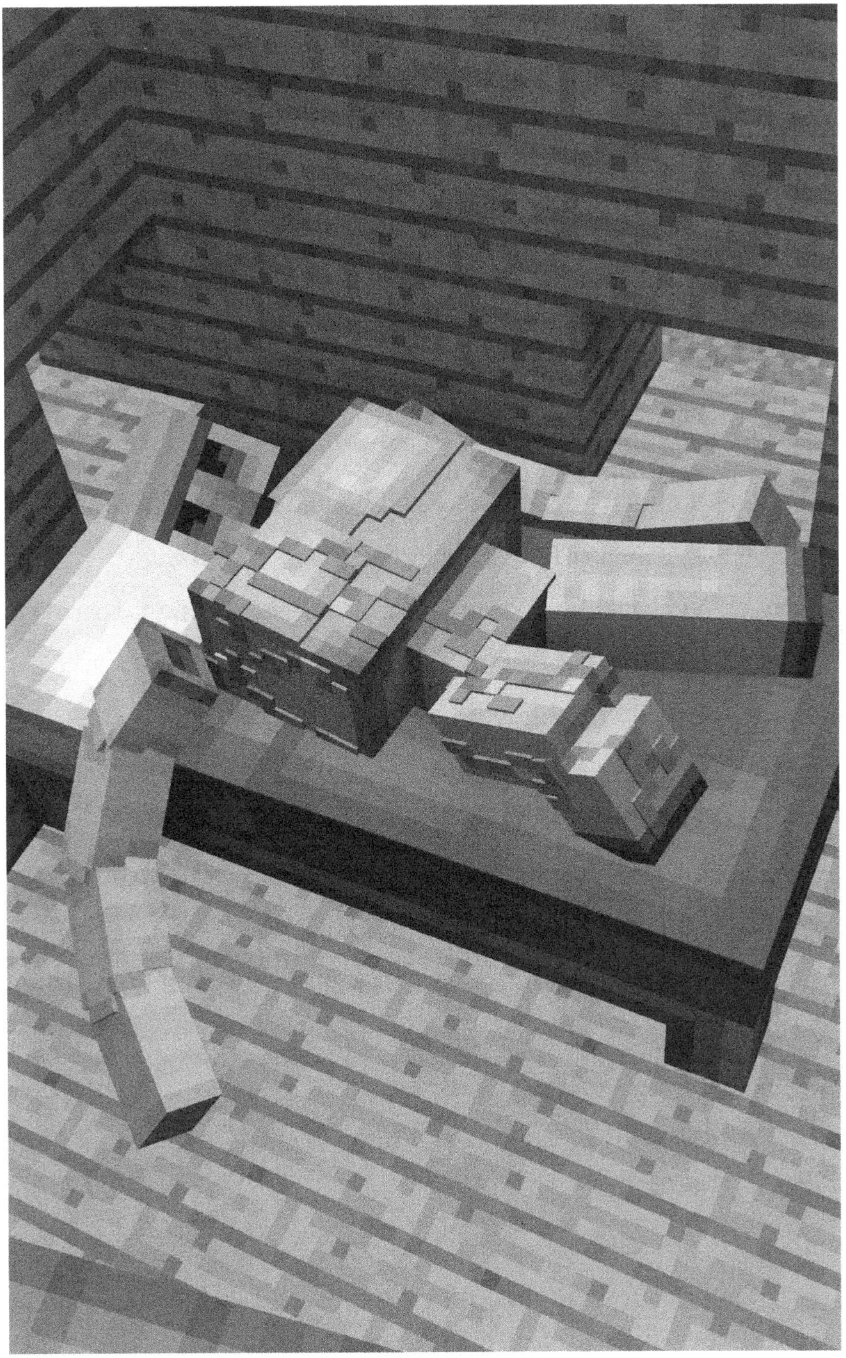

I'm not really feeling that good. I've never seen so many people so angry at me. I've never seen any of them get that angry.

I guess it really was a bad idea—the fireworks. Now, I've destroyed a lot, and people hate me.

Maybe I should just leave.

I sit back up.

Yeah, that's a great idea—a much greater idea than anything else I've thought of before. But maybe I should think about this a bit more, just to be sure.

So, if I go, of course, everyone would be happy. They all made sure I got that a while ago. If I go, I could find another home.

If I stay… Well, maybe I could make up for everything I destroyed, but I'm pretty sure they wouldn't let me. They also made sure I understood that a while ago, too.

I honestly don't see any downside to leaving. Maybe this really *is* a great idea. If I leave, I could have a fresh start. Plus, I don't think anyone will miss me when I'm gone—not after what I just did.

So, it's settled then! Out of this village it is!

I pack up a suitcase—well, a backpack—and take everything I might need for my journey to a new home:

My pickaxe, for several reasons.

A pan because I *do* eat, and to eat, I have to cook, and to cook I need a pan.

A pillow because I *do* sleep, and to sleep, I need a pillow.

A toy animal made of iron because I might get lonely.

A tennis racket because you'll never know when new friends might invite for a game of tennis.

One set of china because you'll never know when you could invite anyone for some tea.

And that's it.

There, I think I'm all set!

I grab all of my stuff and walk to my door—well, the open space where my door should be. I turn back around and look. I try to see if I forgot anything, and I try to memorize the place. I sure am going to miss it.

"Well, goodbye, my house. I hope to see you again in the future," I say before I take a step out.

I don't dare to look back at the village. I keep my head straight and my sight focused right in front of me. I don't need to look back. If I do, I probably won't continue on leaving anymore. I try not to think about it much.

So I keep my focus on walking, putting one foot in front of the other.

"Goodbye, everyone," I say as I leave the village.

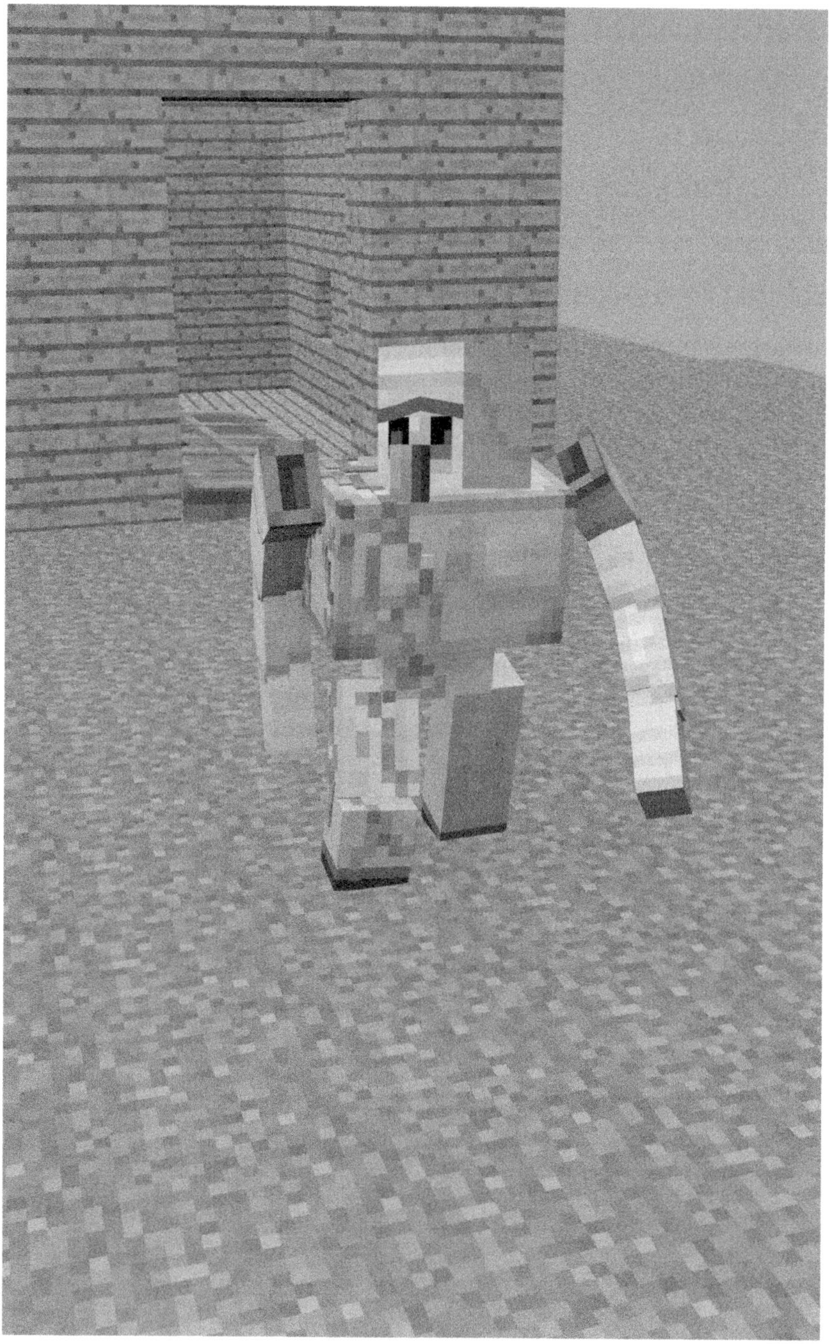

Entry 3

I've been walking for hours now! It's really not that fun anymore. I'm getting pretty tired. I should probably get some rest now. I see a clearing up ahead. That could be a pit stop for me. I quickly run to it and sit on the ground.

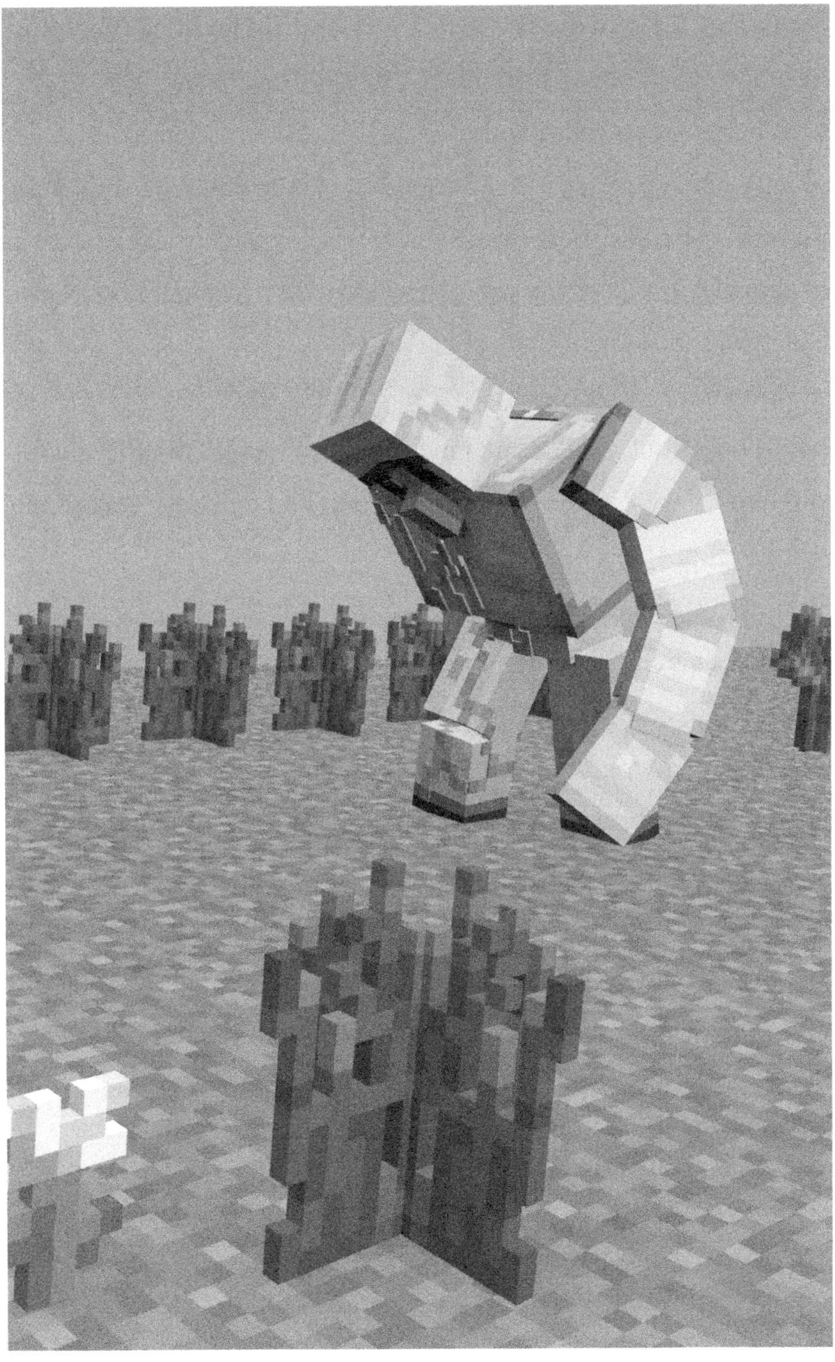

Whew. This feels so much better. I feel like my legs and lungs are burning! I am exhausted! Maybe I can stay for an hour here—you know, just to get reenergized.

I open my backpack and look through it. There could be something here I can use to kill some time.

Oh, actually, I'm pretty thirsty. I'm pretty sure I brought bottles of water with me, so it wouldn't be a problem.

I go through my backpack.

Huh. I don't think I can drink anything in my bag. I might've not brought bottles of water with me. But maybe I can have something to eat instead.

Still nothing. Not even a single piece of candy!

What *do* I even have here?

I pour out the contents of my bag onto the ground.

Well, there's my pickaxe. Hmm, it could be a handy weapon. It could be very useful in the future. Who knows who I could run into? So, at least this one's valid.

Next… A tennis racket.

Why would I have a tennis racket?! What was I thinking? What could I possibly use it for in this journey? Great thinking, Ryder.

China?! A set of china?! Why would I even bother bringing a set of chine to a journey of finding a new home?

Now, moving on.

Oh, what's the point? Everything in here is just useless junk! I don't think I even brought anything that I could actually use. I don't even have food to eat! I did bring a pan, but I didn't even bring anything I could cook *in* the pan!

I sigh.

At least I have a pillow. I put it on the ground and gently lay my head on it.

Ooh, that feels good.

Maybe I could just sleep the discomfort and thirst away. Then I'll have enough energy to get to the next village by tonight.

Yep, sleep will be great.

I close my eyes.

I hear a low rumble from the skies. My eyes open involuntarily. The skies have darkened. A large dark cloud floats above me.

That looks like a big storm.

I hope that doesn't fall on me.

And, of course, I spoke too soon.

Raindrops start to drop on my face one by one, slowly. Thunder crashes in the distance yet again.

I quickly gather my stuff and put them back into my backpack. Of course, everything in it is useless, but I still wouldn't want them to get wet.

The raindrops are getting bigger. It's really starting to rain. I've got to get out of here. I've got to find some place where I can keep myself dry.

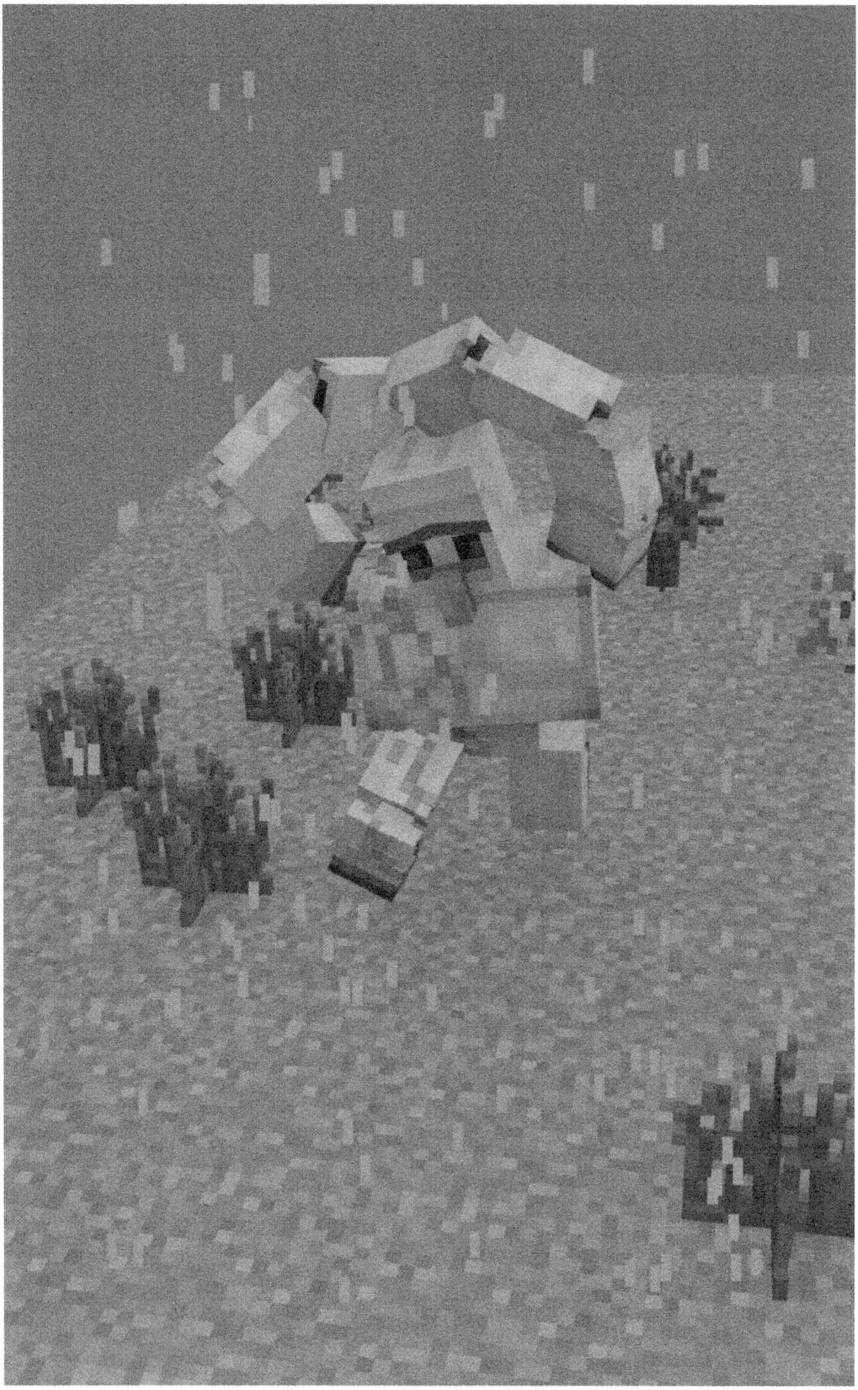

Where could I possibly find a place like that out here in the middle of the woods?

The rain is getting stronger. I hear thunder yet again. The sky is getting even darker.

I pick up my bag and start to run. I don't know where I'm going, but I'm just going to keep running. I'd go anywhere to keep myself dry. But I don't think that's going to happen anymore. The rain is pouring, the sky is lit up by lightning, and strong winds are blowing against me as I run.

I didn't even have the brains to pack up my umbrella!

Well, in my defense, it was a pretty good day this morning. The sky was clear and blue. Who would've thought that it would rain this hard?!

Ugh. And now I'm wet. Everywhere I run, there's just trees and it's really not helping me stay dry. How I hope there will be some lone house or cabin nearby.

It's freezing! Oh, what I'd do for some fire right now!

I continue to run with my arms crossed against my chest, trying to squeeze away the chills. I take back everything I said about hating summer and heat and sweat. I'd give my arms to feel warm right now.

The sun is starting to set. It's getting dark. I have to find somewhere to stay! I can't just stand around getting myself rained on.

How I wish some shelter would magically appear in front of me. I've been running for almost an hour now. I'm tired, hungry, and soaking wet.

This clearly isn't the best idea.

Wait, I think that's a cave. Well, it looks like a cave. I just hope it really is one with a warm wide space inside and no monsters around. I run towards it. It's like a huge hole in a huge rock. It *is* a cave, alright. But it's completely dark inside.

I think I'd rather stay outside.

Suddenly, thunder booms just as a flash of lightning lights up the sky.

I run straight into the darkness that is the empty void in the center of the cave. I can't see a thing! I feel like I'm blind. Maybe I *am* blind. Maybe I should get back out—or at least stay near the cave's entrance. Maybe some moonlight could help me get my sight back. Carefully and with much caution, I slowly step back from where I came from. I stand near the entrance of the cave. It's still pretty dark because of the rain clouds, I suppose. But I can see little bits and pieces of the outside world.

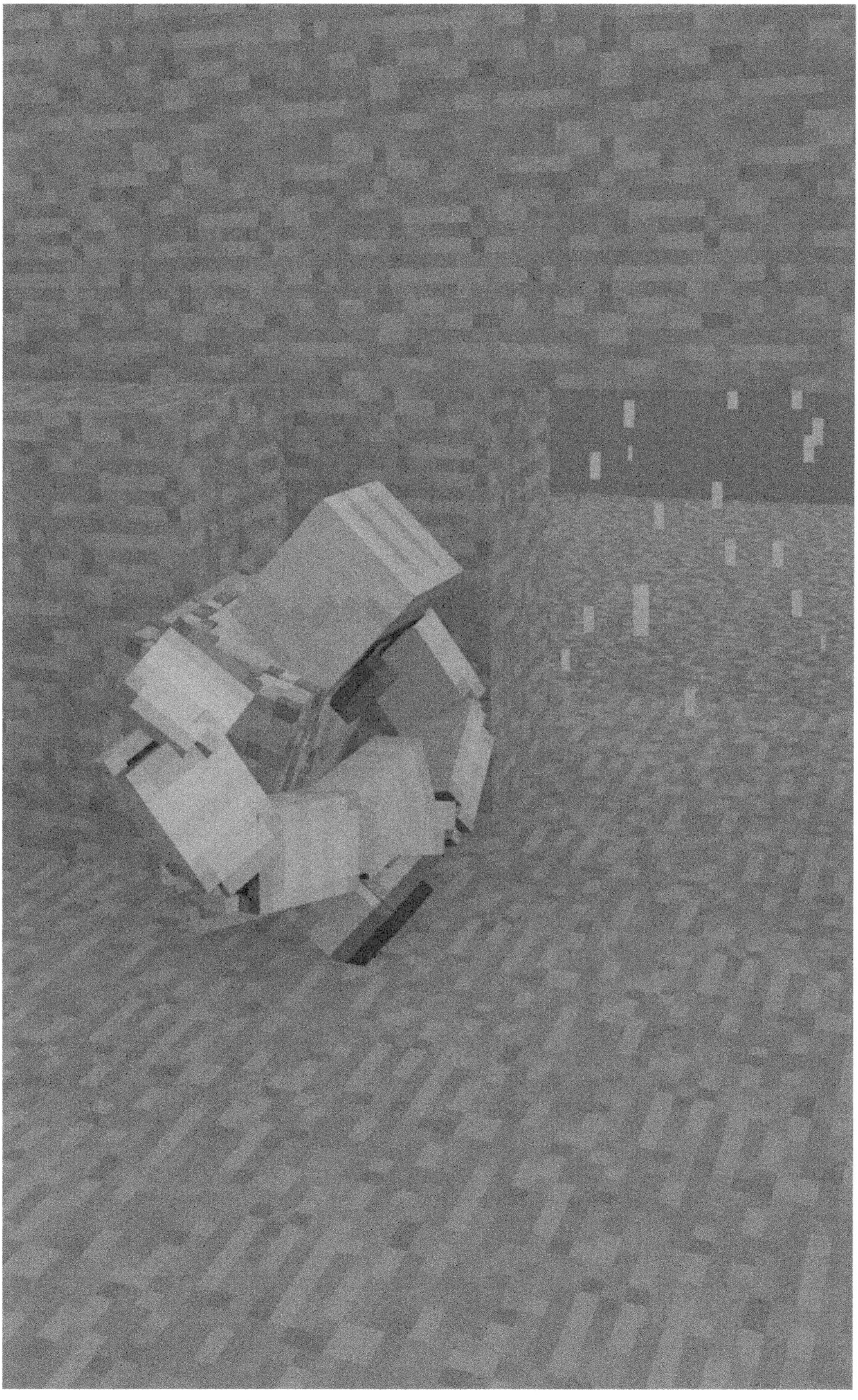

Whew. At least I'm sure I'm not blind.

I may have pretty poor eyesight right now, but at least I have a roof over my head. At least I've got that going for me, which is nice.

I sit on the ground, which is thankfully dry. I can hear the rain pouring outside.

I guess I'd have to stay here for a while. Maybe I should just sleep. Yeah, that would be great.

I pull out my pillow from my backpack. I lay my head on the soft pillow and closed my eyes. Boy, do I feel tired!

At least the pillow wasn't such a terrible idea.

But everything else is.

I'm still not sure if I should've run away. I'm tired, hungry, and soaking wet. But I'm here—I've already left.

Maybe tomorrow will be better.

Entry 4

Wow. My bed is hard and very uncomfortable. I'm pretty sure I made the bed last night.

I look up at my ceiling. Wait, that's not my ceiling. That's a rock.

I sit up. I look around. I'm surrounded by rock.

Why am I inside a rock?!

Did I shrink last night and then ended up in a rock?! Am I the size of an ant now?! How am I supposed to go back to my normal size? How am I going to get out of this rock?!

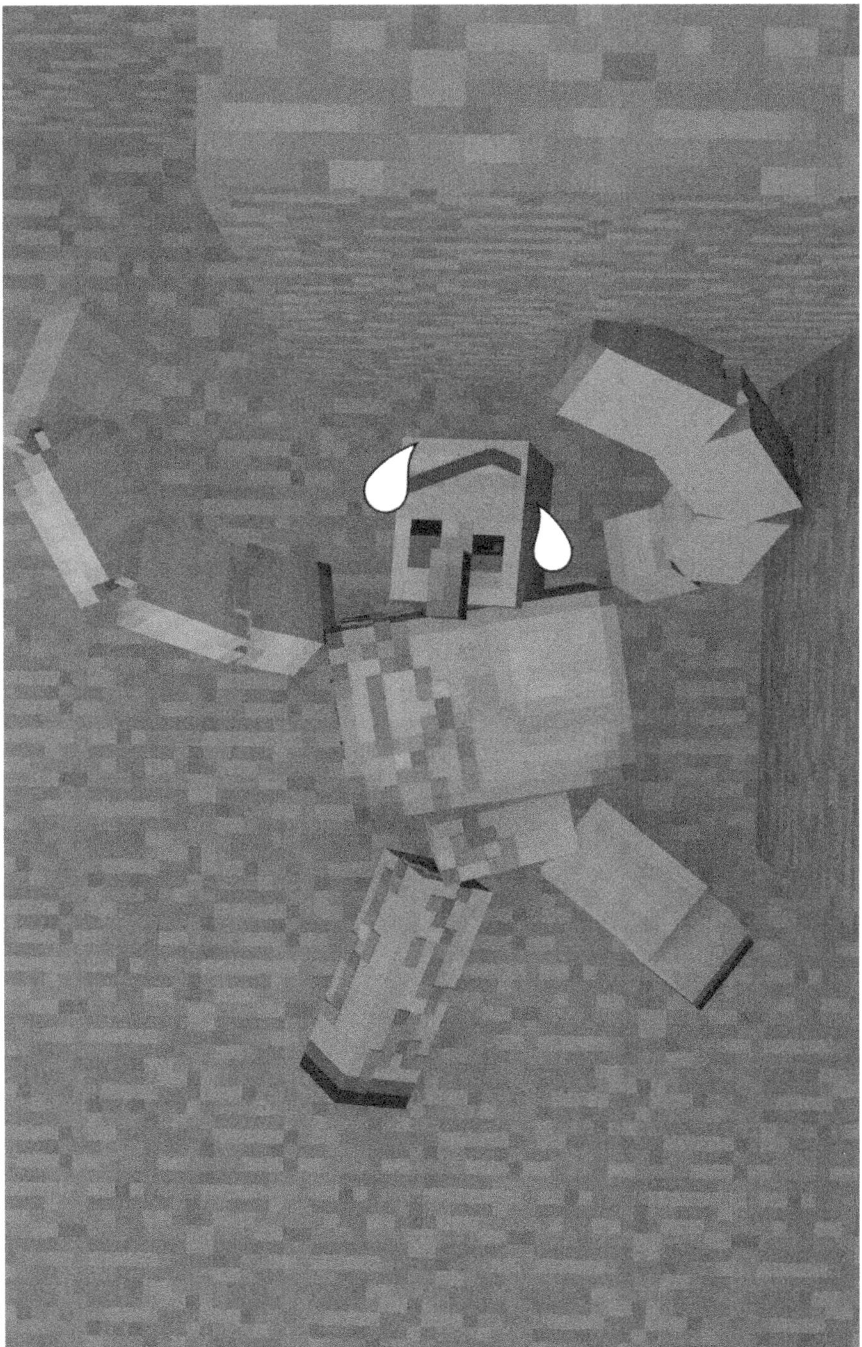

I turn around.

Oh, there's the exit.

I pick up my pillow and backpack and head out. I find myself in the middle of some kind of forest and in front of some kind of cave.

Right. I was caught in a downpour last night and slept in a cave. That was the rock thing.

Whew. At least I'm still in normal size. Maybe now I should go on with my journey. I wouldn't want to be caught up in a storm again—even though the skies are actually clear now. But who knows? It was this way yesterday.

Anyway, I really should be back on my way.

So I head to the trail and follow it.

I wonder how far the next town is.

Hmm…What time is it? The sky is already getting dark. I must have woke up super late in the evening because I was totally drained from yesterday.

I think I hear footsteps—hundreds of footsteps, actually. It seems like a mob is walking somewhere near. It sounds like a huge crowd is just marching around the trail.

What could that be?

The footsteps are getting louder. I could also hear some chattering and hollering and yelling. It actually sounds pretty scary.

I take cover behind a tree and watch. The crowd, or mob, or whatever it is, seems to be getting closer.

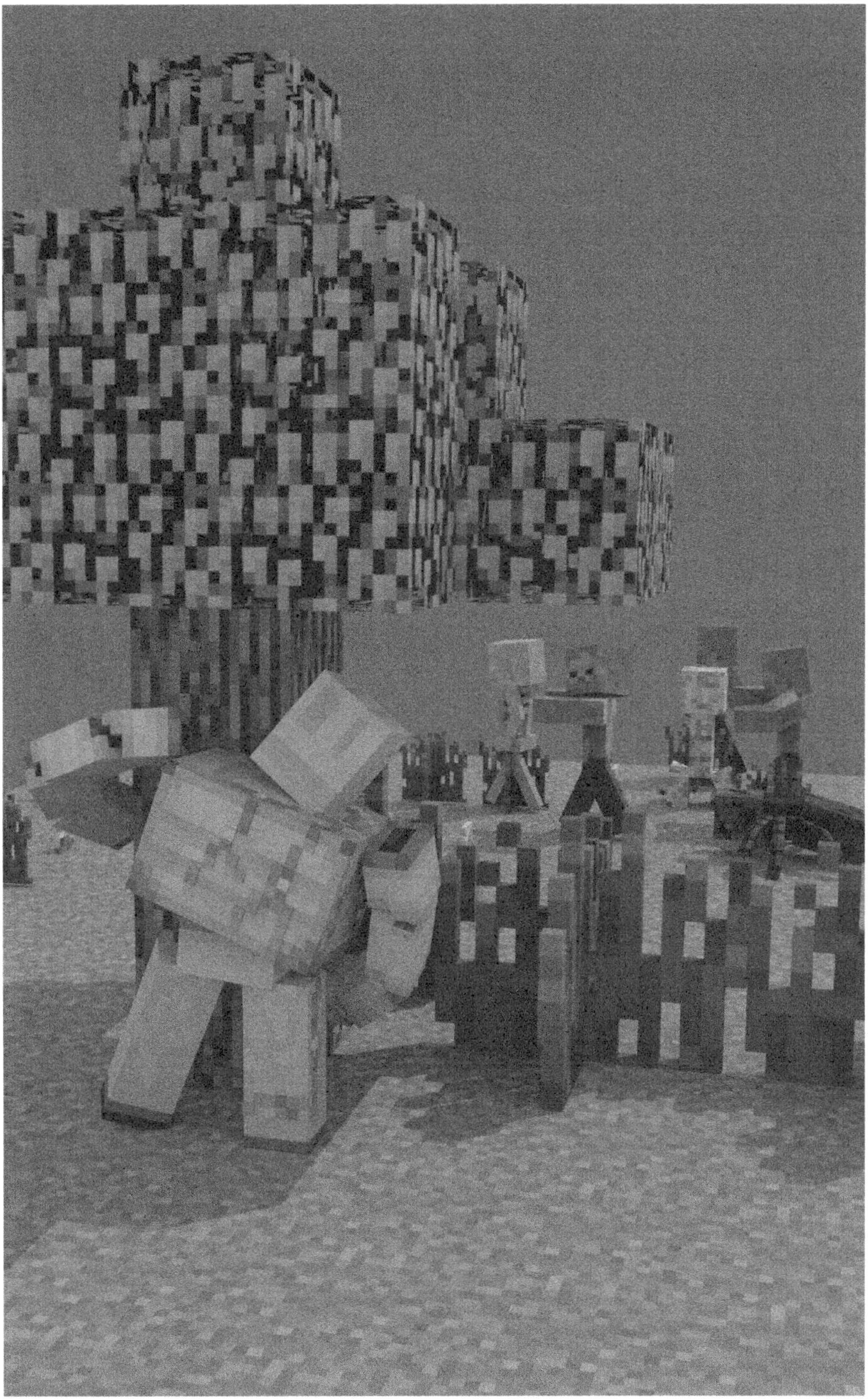

Whoa.

Those are zombies… *and* monsters. And they're making their way on the trail.

My mouth drops open.

It's a mob of zombies and monsters! I couldn't believe it. I haven't seen any yet; this is the first time. They look pretty normal, to be honest—the difference is just that they're undead. This is so awesome!

I should probably take a step forward—see them closer.

I move to another tree that's closer to the trail. The pack—or maybe they're called herd?—of zombies walks right in front of me.

They all look hungry. Plus, where could they be going? Do they really travel in such big groups? Why don't they have anything, any luggage or baggage with them?

I move closer.

Snap!

Whoops. I just stepped on a branch. The sound is loud enough to take the zombies' attention. They all turn their heads towards me.

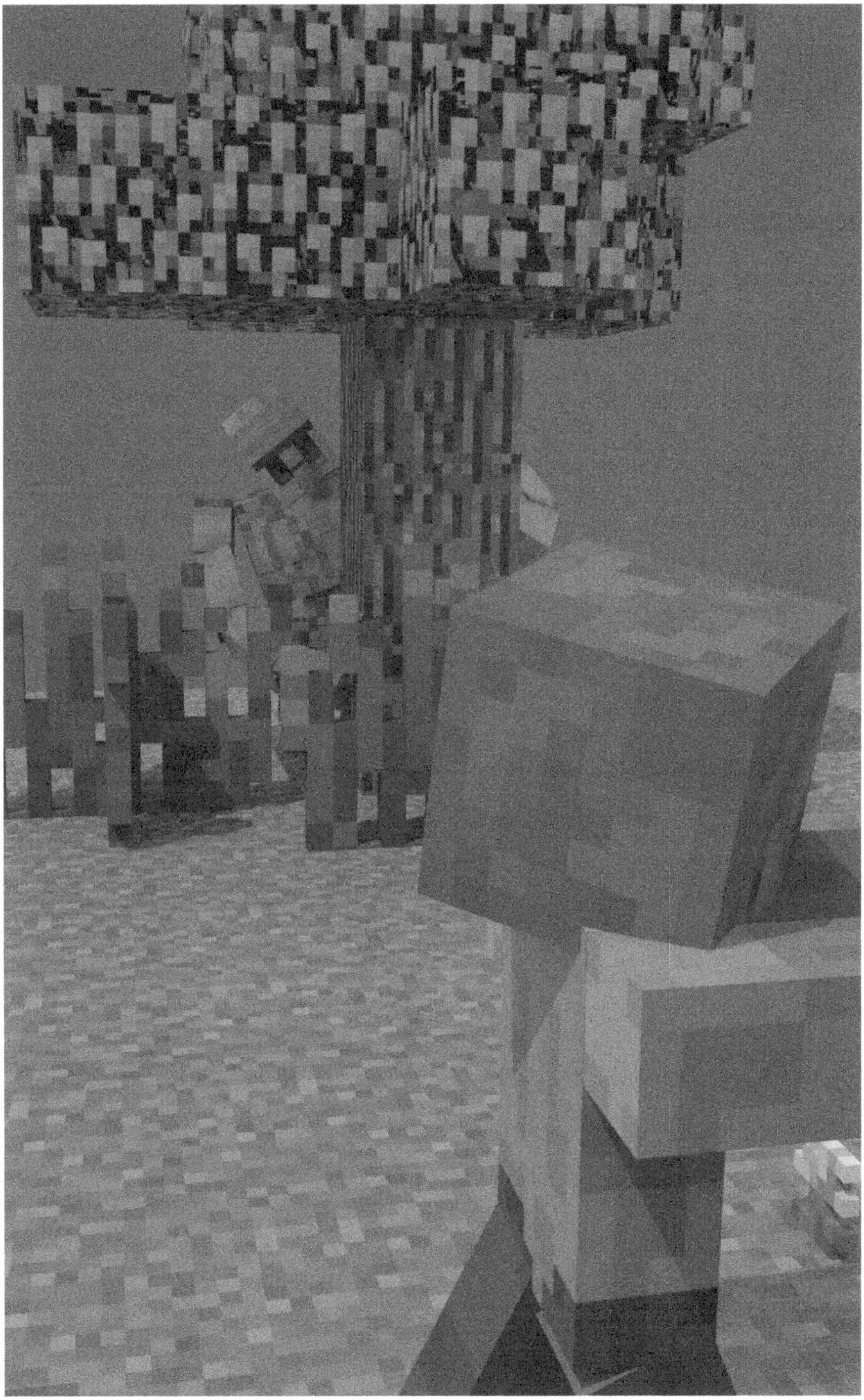

I'm going to be dead.

I mean, I did say that they looked normal, but they're still zombies and monsters who eat people's brains. Now, with their eyes on me, I'm pretty sure I'm in danger. I shouldn't have moved closer.

Because now, *they're* moving closer.

I could run, but I'm pretty sure one of them could easily outrun me and catch me and then eat my brains.

Still, I could. But I can't seem to move my legs, or any other part of my body for that matter. I just feel like if I move, they'll pounce on me and just rip out my brain. I need my brain! I don't want it to be food for these monsters!

So, I stay in place and watch. I wait and watch as the mob of zombies and monsters slowly move towards me. They move closer until they are just a few feet away from me. They could easily grab hold of me from where I'm standing.

This is it. This is the end of Ryder the iron golem.

This is what I get for leaving a perfectly good life in the village. I am going to get eaten by zombies and monsters. I wouldn't even be able to last two days outside the village!

And now they are right in front of me.

A zombie is standing just inches away from me. He's probably the chosen one to rip my brains out.

He opens his mouth.

This is it. My dreams of becoming a world-champion in food eating *and* becoming a horse-trainer is about to be gone.

Oh, how I wish it would be quick and fast. I'm not strong enough to endure the pain of having no brain in my skull.

I close my eyes and wait for my final doom. I wait for the pain.

"Hey there. Are you lost?" instead came a voice.

Oh, that must be the angel that must take me to my final place.

I slowly open my eyes to peek.

Whoa. That's no angel. It's still the zombie. The zombie is still in front of me, but now he's… smiling?

I open both of my eyes. Apparently, I'm still on the ground and the mob has surrounded me, but none of them is making a move to touch me.

My eyebrows furrow.

Is this really happening? So I am still alive?

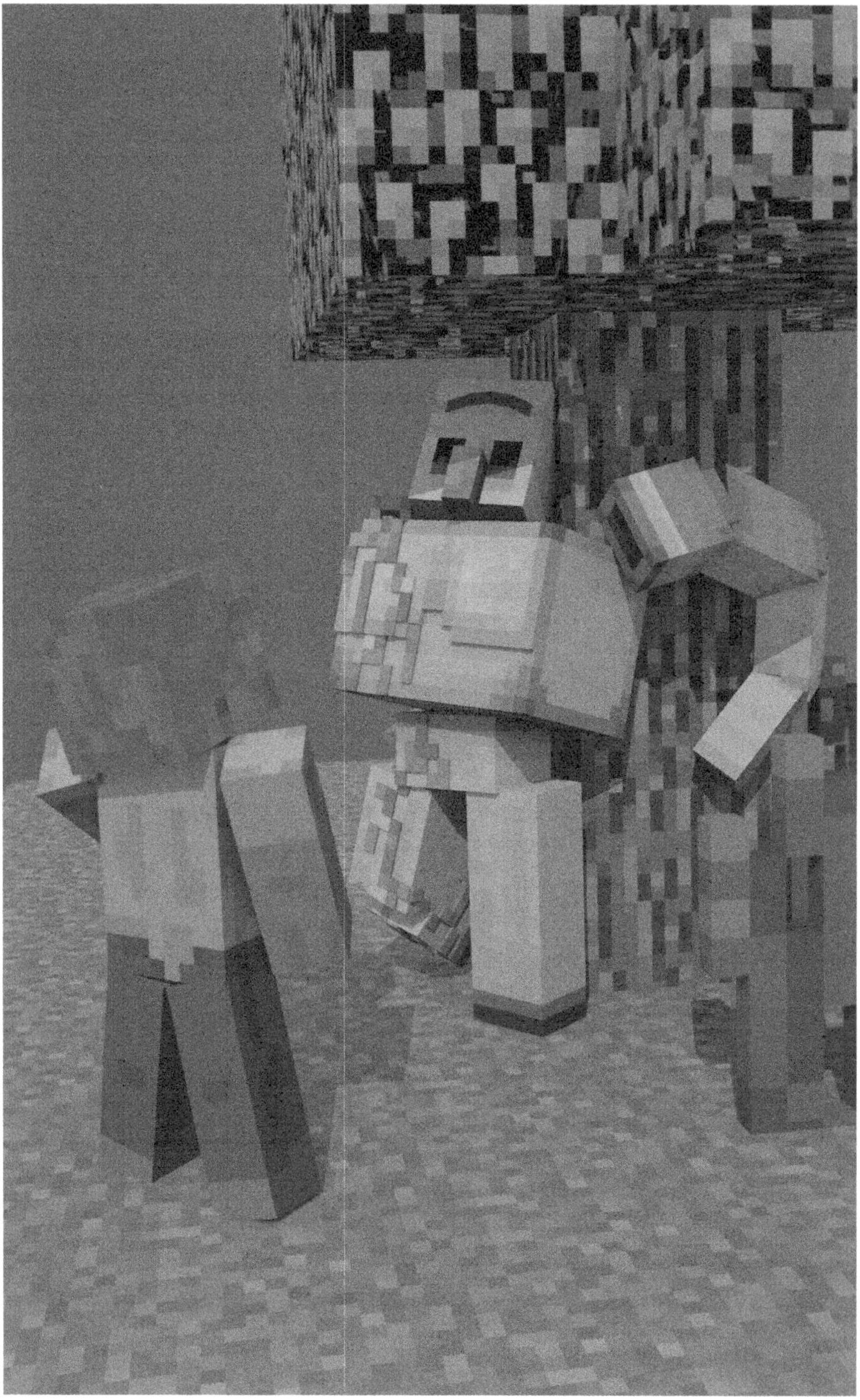

"Hey, iron golem. Are you lost?" asks the zombie, the supposed predator.

Could he be talking to me?

I look around, but there aren't any other iron golems around.

"Are you talking to me?" I ask.

The zombie laughs. "Of course! Who else would I be talking to? You're the only iron golem around here!" He then turns to his fellows surrounding us. "I think he could be pretty lost up here," he says as he points to his skull.

Everyone laughs hysterically.

I don't get it.

I would ask what the joke was, but I had bigger issues to face.

"Aren't you going to eat me? Or at least eat my brain?" I ask the zombie.

Again, they all laugh.

I still don't get the joke.

"What? Why would I eat you? Or your brain? That's ridiculous!" he answers.

That's confusing. "Well, you're zombies and monsters! Don't you eat brains and people?" I say.

These monsters can't seem to stop laughing.

"Yes, we do. But you're not a villager! We only eat villagers and villagers' brains," he explains. "Besides, I don't think I'll be satisfied with yours." I notice him grin and raise his eyebrows at the zombies behind him.

They laugh yet again. It must be some kind of inside joke.

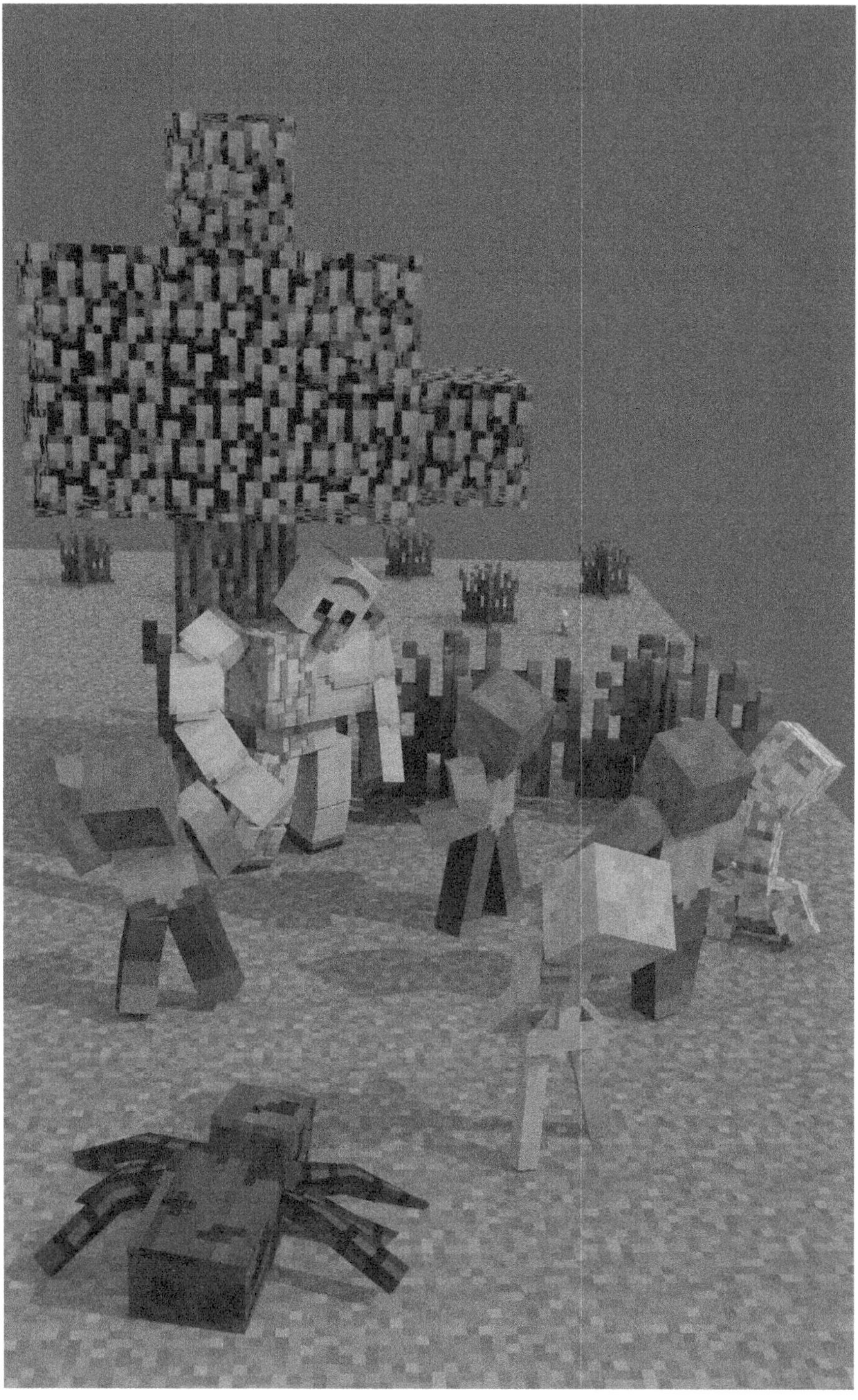

But anyway, at least now I wouldn't have to worry about them eating me or my brain.

"So, you're not going to eat me?" I ask again, just to be sure. You can never be too sure.

"Of course not!" the zombies and monsters answer.

Whew! That's a relief! I guess I still have a chance at becoming the world-champion at food eating. Oh, there is just so much to live for!

"So, where are you heading?" asks a monster. "It's unlikely for an iron golem like you to be roaming around the woods."

"I'm going to the next village. I'm going to live there now," I explain.

The zombies and monsters nod. I think they can relate to me.

"The next village is miles away—it would probably take us a day to get there," declares a monster. "Why don't you join us? We're on our way there, anyway."

I stare at them with wide eyes. Did a real life zombie just really invite me to travel with them?

"Really? Wow, thank you!" I say. It is going to be a real treat to be travelling with new friends—it's no fun to travel all alone. So this is definitely one thing I am not going to pass up.

"Of course! Now let's go and get ready to continue on with our journey," says a monster.

The mob then goes back to the trail and heads in the direction that they were going to a while ago—but this time, I'm with them.

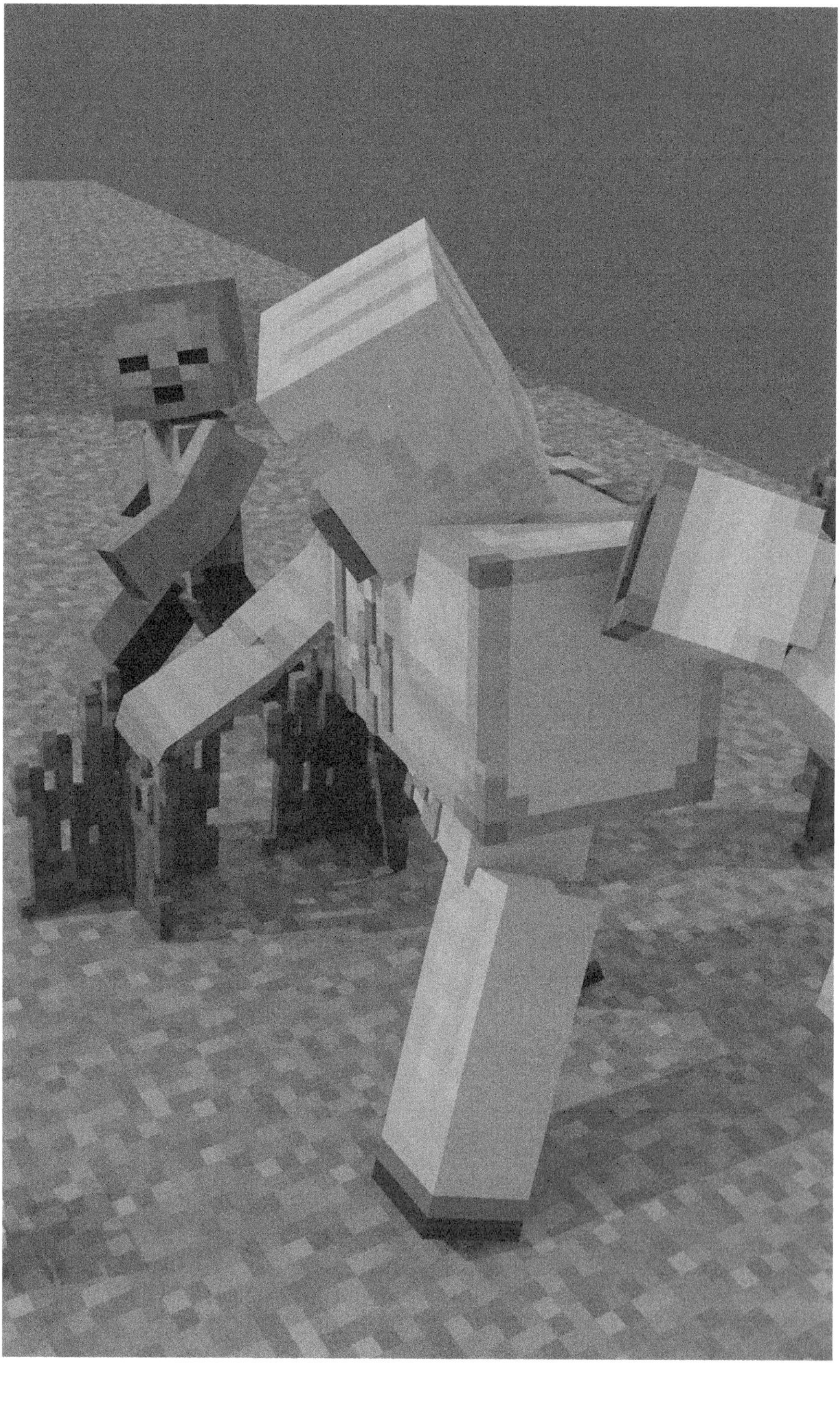

Entry 5

We've been walking for hours, but amazingly, it feels like we've just been walking for a few minutes.

We're having so much fun! At least, I am. The zombies and monsters are all very welcoming. We've been talking and talking about everything! They've been telling me stories about the villages that they've visited. They've been all over the world! It all sounds so exciting.

"How 'bout you, Ryder?" one of them asks. "What's your story?"

Everyone turns to look at me.

"What do you mean?" I say.

"Tell us about yourself. Why are you travelling to the next village, anyway?"

"Oh. Well, it's kind of a long story," I say. I'm not sure I'm ready to tell them the story of my life. Too much has happened to push me to my situation now. It really is a long story to explain.

"Let me guess," says the zombie. "You destroyed your village and ran away from home to find a new one."

Huh?

"Oh, wow. I guess it isn't that long of a story," I say. That pretty much explains everything. "But yes, you're right! That's amazing. How did you know about that? Are you some kind of fortune teller? Or one of those physics?"

The zombie laughs. "Do you mean 'psychics'? I'm not. I just know what you are."

I frown. "And what am I?"

"An iron golem, of course!" he answers. "That means that you have the tendency of destroying things. Am I right?"

My eyes widen. This is awesome! How did he know that?!

"Yes! That's true! How did you know that? You *are* a physic, aren't you?" I exclaim. "I *do* destroy lots of things, and that's why I'm going to move to another village. I'm pretty sure the villagers want to have nothing to do with me. They probably haven't even noticed that I'm gone. When they do, they'd most definitely have some kind of party to celebrate. They all hate me!"

"Now, now," says Mike, one of the zombies. I feel like he's one of the leaders of the group. He just has that aura with him. "Don't be too hard on yourself. You're an iron golem! You guys just really have a knack for destroying things. I don't know why, but I'm pretty sure it's innate in you guys. I've met lots of iron golems before, and they all had the same problem as yours. That's why I think you'll be a great addition to our group."

"What?" I ask. Did Mike just tell me what I think I heard? Was that an invitation to join them and travel with them all around the world?

"Join us. Join us in our trips to different villages!" Mike says.

My eyes widen. I couldn't believe my ears. They *did* just ask me to come with them! How can I pass up on this? This is going to be awesome!

"I will! Oh, wow! Yes, yes!" I exclaim.

Everyone cheers.

Wow, so that's how great it feels to have people cheer for you. This is the first time, and it feels so amazing.

"But I hope you understand what we do to the villages," Mike says. "We hunt villagers. What you said a while ago is true. We *do* eat villagers' brains. When we raid villages, that's what we do. We don't just waltz in and go sight-seeing. We destroy villages."

"Oh," I say.

I should've thought of that.

"Are you okay with that?" asks Mike.

I feel all eyes on me.

Am I okay with that?

"Well, I *have* destroyed a village. So, that's a start. And… I think I'm okay with it," I say.

Everyone cheers again.

"Welcome to our family, Ryder," says Mike.

I'm welcomed with hugs and pats on the back. I've never met people who like me this much! I've never felt so accepted in my whole life! I could really enjoy this. I feel so alive already! I feel like this is just exactly where I'm supposed to be. My running away wasn't such a terrible idea after all! I feel like it could even be the best idea I've ever had.

Now, my life is going to change for sure.

"We're here!" someone from the front of our group exclaims.

We all stop. We're just right outside the entrance of the village. It doesn't look exactly like the village back home, but there *are* similarities.

Mike turns to me. "Alright, Ryder. You ready to experience your new life?"

I nod eagerly. "I am more than ready! So what's the plan? What do I do? Do we wear black ninja outfits?"

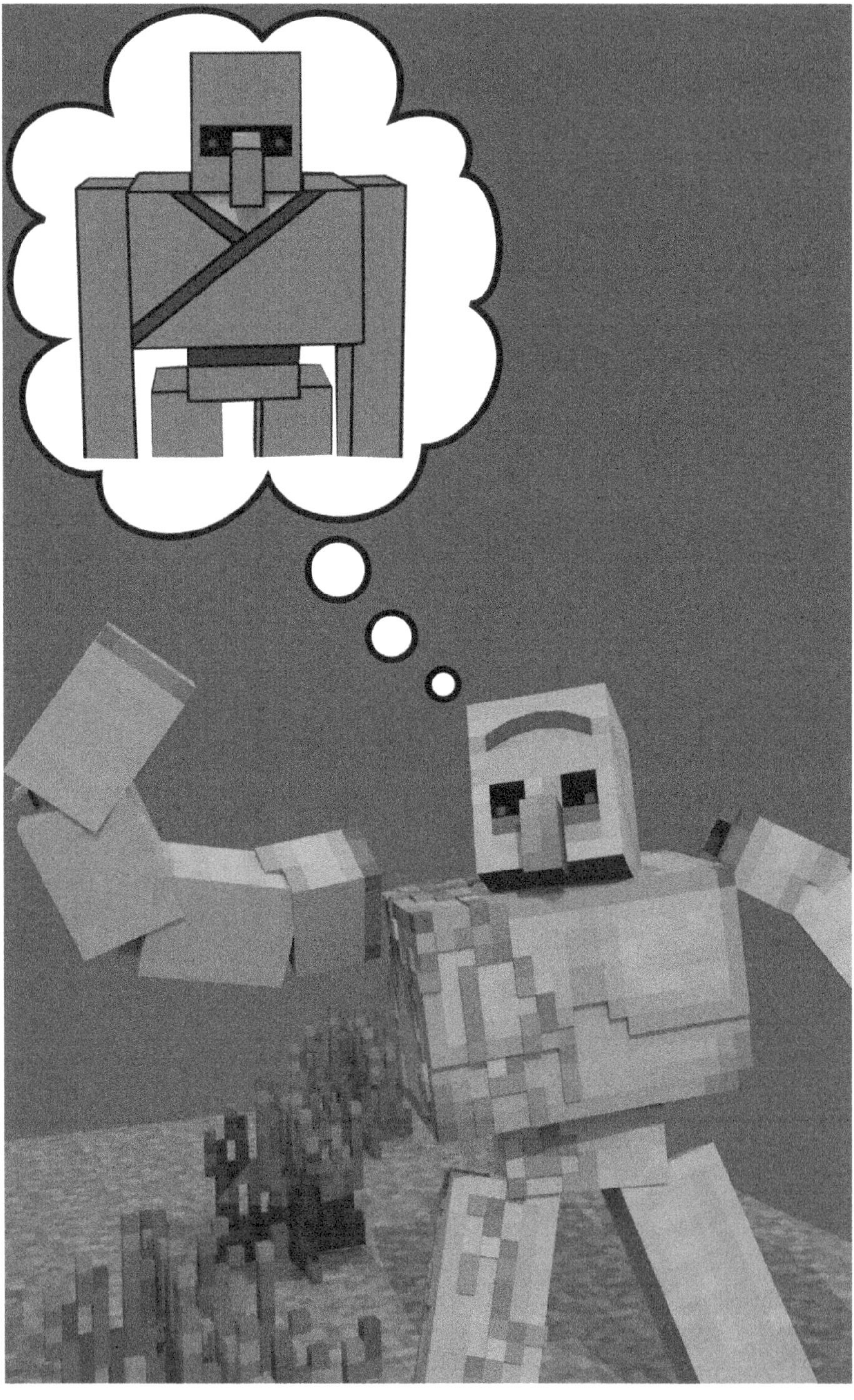

Mike chuckles. "No, we don't. We're not ninjas."

"Oh." That's a bit of a downer. I've always wanted to wear a ninja outfit.

"We just go in there and get some food—ours *and* yours. So, just do what you want and make sure that we all have food to eat," Mike says with a pat on my shoulder.

I nod. "Alright. I understand."

"If things get a little too gory for you to take, you can always look away," he adds. "But you'll get used to it."

He turns to the other zombies and monsters.

"Let's go!" Mike exclaims.

The whole mob starts running towards the village. I am with them, too, of course. This is it! This is my new life now.

It's awesome how these guys can make no sound as they run towards the village. That's probably why they don't need any ninja costumes. No one would even expect them until these brain-eating zombies and monsters are already knocking at these villagers' doors.

The village is quiet. The villagers are all going about their business, not knowing the chaos that is about to happen.

And then suddenly, zombies and monsters—and an iron golem; that's me—hit the village like a storm.

I see the riot unravel right before my very eyes. Every zombie and monster pounced on villagers and ripped out their brains like there's no tomorrow. Then they'd move on to other victims.

I'm left here standing with my feet firmly on the ground, trying to figure out what to do next. It's my first time to witness something like this, and Mike was right, it *is* a little bit gory. But it's not too much—I can take it. I just have to figure out how to move my legs and what my next step is.

Mike said to just make sure that everyone gets to eat. How do I do that? Oh, maybe I've got something in my bag that could help.

I look inside the backpack. A pan!

I pull it out. "I've got a pan!" I exclaim as I swing it up above my head.

Bang!

Something hard just hit my pan. I turn around.

A villager is lying on the ground, unconscious.

Whoops. My bad.

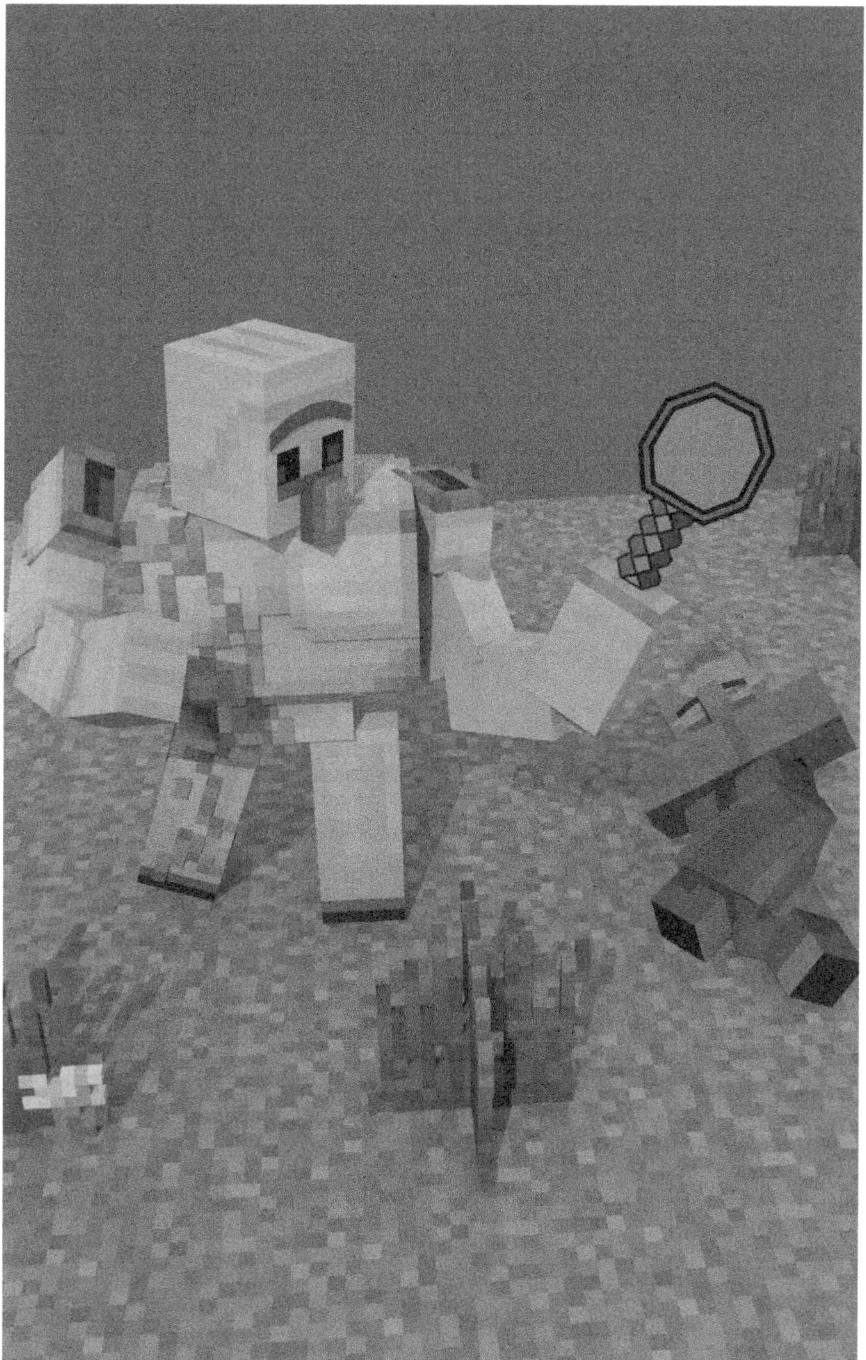

He really shouldn't be standing within my area. He should know that bad things happen around me.

Now a zombie is running towards me. He's probably going to scold me for what I did.

"Oh, hey! You got him! Good job!" the zombie says. "This one was a runner. Thanks!" Then he goes on and rips out the villager's brain.

Huh. I actually got appreciation for destroying someone. That's definitely a first. But I'm not going to complain. I have to admit, it feels great to be appreciated!

This life is definitely going to be so much fun.

The screams from villagers continue, but I don't think I really mind. Now I just want to make sure that we—my new zombie and monster family—would be able to get what we came here for.

And now I'm hungry.

I go to the nearest house I can find and try the door.

Locked.

But I've seen this before—I've heard stories about this. I can just pick the lock! Now if I could just find something in my backpack that can pick this lock…

Aha! My pickaxe! The name itself has the word 'pick' in it. I believe this is it.

I slam the pickaxe into the doorknob. Whoops. It drops right out of the door, and then the door swings open easily.

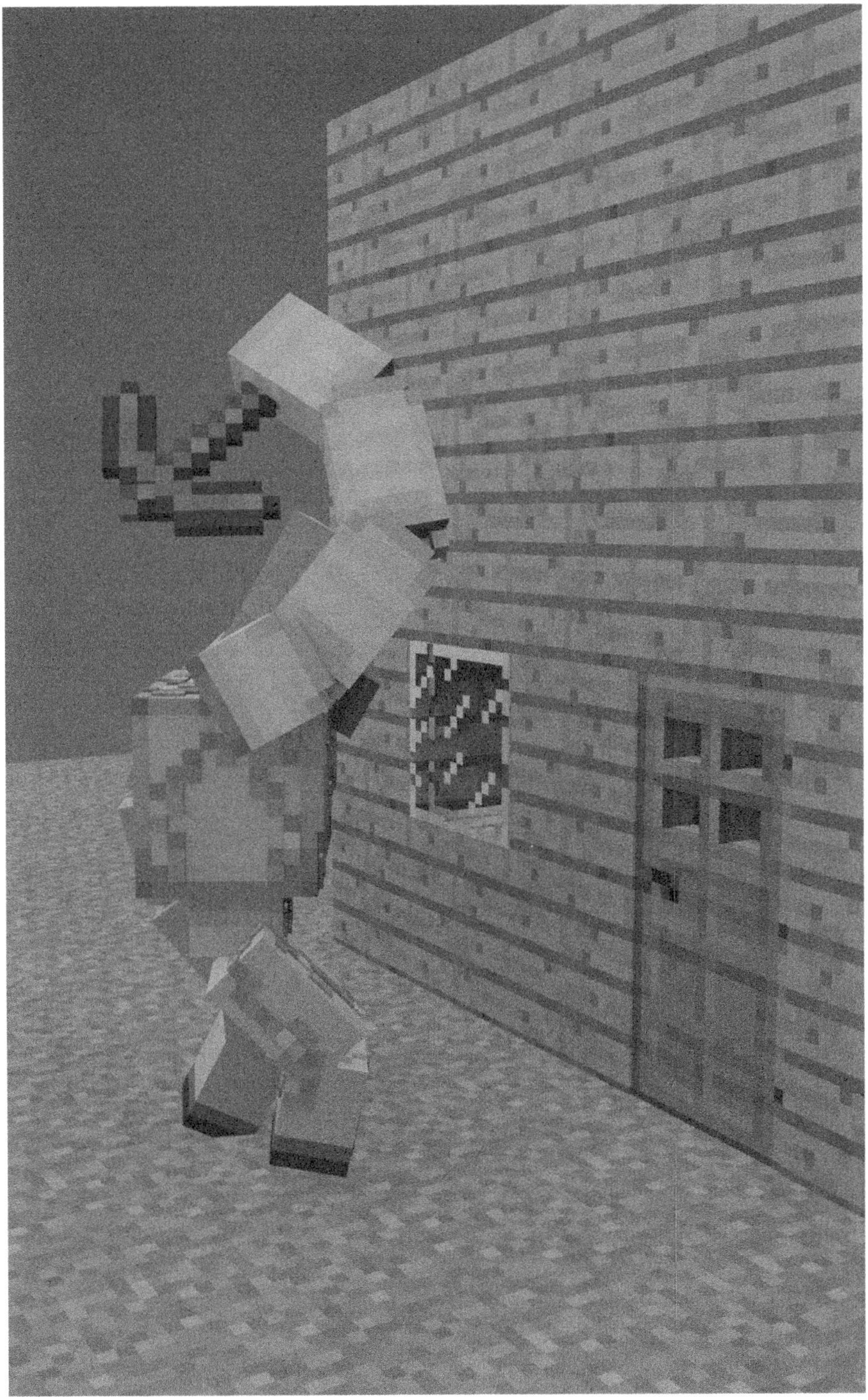

That was easy.

I walk into the house and go straight to the kitchen.

Wow. This house is loaded up! I take a bite from the cake on the counter.

That is amazing. I can't remember the last time I've tasted something like this. The zombies and monsters need to taste this.

Wait, do they even eat villagers' food? Never mind, I'll just eat it if they don't want it.

I look around the kitchen and take out some plastic containers that I can put food in.

Oh, here they are. And there's soup on the furnace, too. Maybe I should reheat it first before taking it. I wouldn't want to eat cold soup.

I turn the fire of the furnace up to full blast.

That should do it.

In the meantime, I'm going to load up on fruits and vegetables. It doesn't hurt to eat healthy. Maybe I could even lose a pound or two.

I put apples, potatoes, and bunches of carrots into my bag.

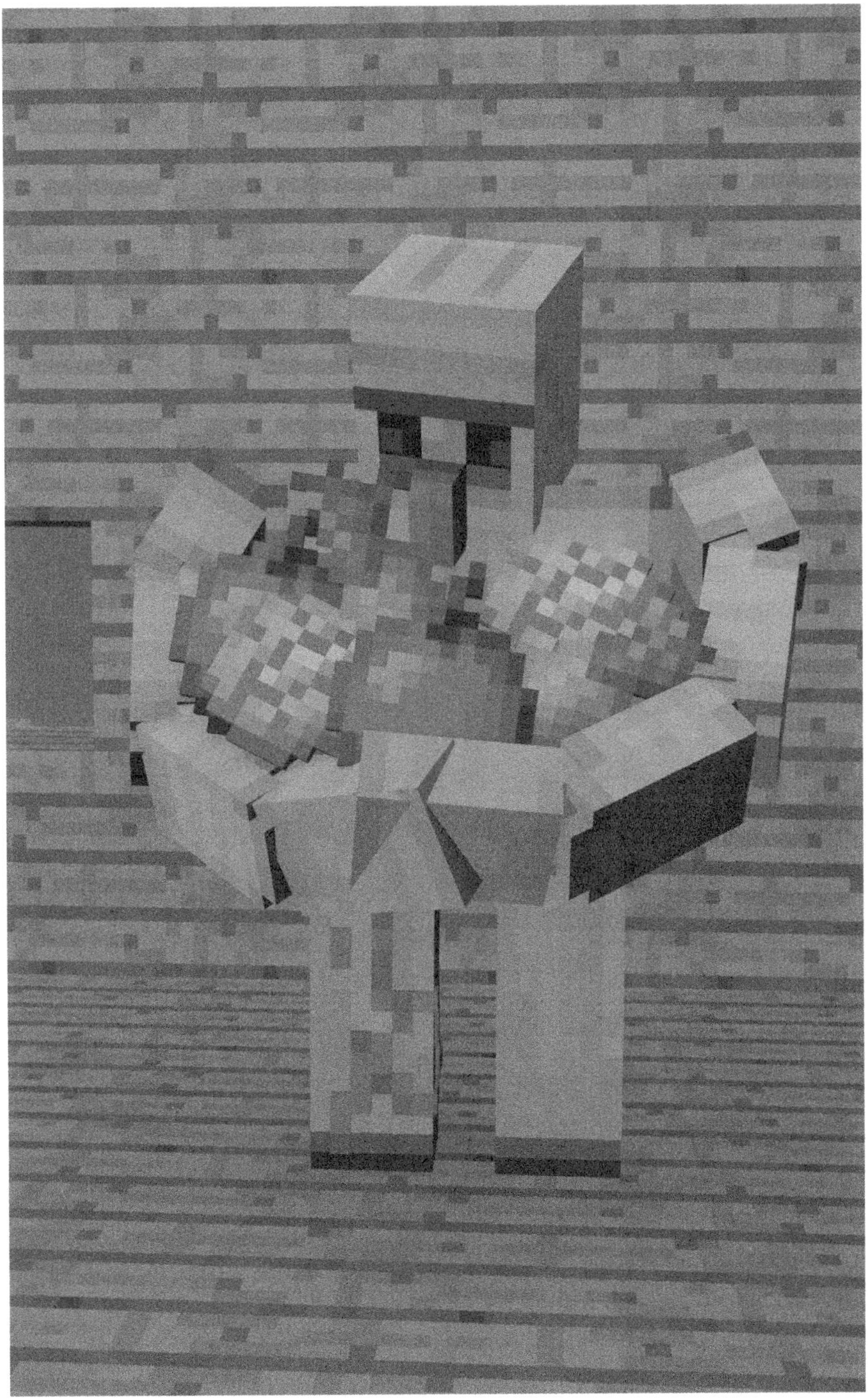

Eeeeeeeeeeeee!

Something's whistling. What could it be?

Ooh! There's chocolate!

Bang!

Whoa. What was that?

The lid of the soup pot is gone.

I look around. Just a few feet away from me, there's a villager lying on the floor. And the pot lid is lying beside him, too.

Wow, it must've hit the villager and knocked him out.

A zombie suddenly runs in and starts chomping on the villager. Then the zombie looks at me, "Thanks, bro!" Then he continues to eat.

Well, at least someone else is happy.

I go back to the kitchen and start to pack up more food. This is going to last me for weeks! I love this new life.

I run out the house with bags of food in my hands. Outside, most of the zombies and monsters are already finishing up. The screams are getting softer. I think everyone else is already full. At least I've got mountains of food.

There are bodies of villagers lying around. I have to admit, it does need a little bit of getting used to. But I think I *could* have a little bit of fun with this. After years with this family, I'm pretty sure I'll get used to it.

This is the most fun I've had since… forever! Back home, every little mistake I made always grew bigger and would explode in my face. But here, now, I could accidentally knock out a villager and still be praised!

What iron golem wouldn't want that?!

This is *definitely* the best idea I've ever had. I've said that many times before. But this time, it's true.

I see groups of zombies and monsters heading back towards the trail. I guess we're all heading back.

Mike suddenly appears beside me.

"Are you guys done?" I ask him.

"Yeah, a few of us are just finishing up," he answers. "What about you? Have you had your fill?"

"Absolutely. I even got some spare. You know, just in case we run out of villages," I say as I hold up my backpack.

Mike chuckles. "Nice job! But you really don't need to do that. There's plenty of villages in the world! We'll never run out. Unless you really eat a lot."

I grin. I probably look like a pig to him.

"So what's next?" I ask.

He smiles. "We head back home."

"Home?" I have a new home now? I actually have a place to really call home? One that will accept me?

Wow.

"Yeah. It's going to be quite a walk, but we'll get there soon enough," Mike says.

"Great!" I say. "Can't wait."

"I think everyone's already heading back," he says. "We should go, too."

I nod. We start heading for the trail where the others are already waiting.

"So, you got lots of food," Mike says. "Did you have any trouble?"

"Actually, I didn't. It's like the food just came to me. It was awesome!" I say excitedly. I must look like some overly excited kid that just came back from the candy store.

"So you had fun?"

"Of course! I've never had that much fun in years! In forever, actually! Normally, I'd get in trouble for everything that happened back there. But here, it's okay."

Mike smiles. "Of course it is! I'm glad you had fun," he says. "So... you're staying with us?"

I look at him and smile. I don't need to think about it. I already know the answer.

"Yes, of course, I'm staying," I say. "Let's go home."

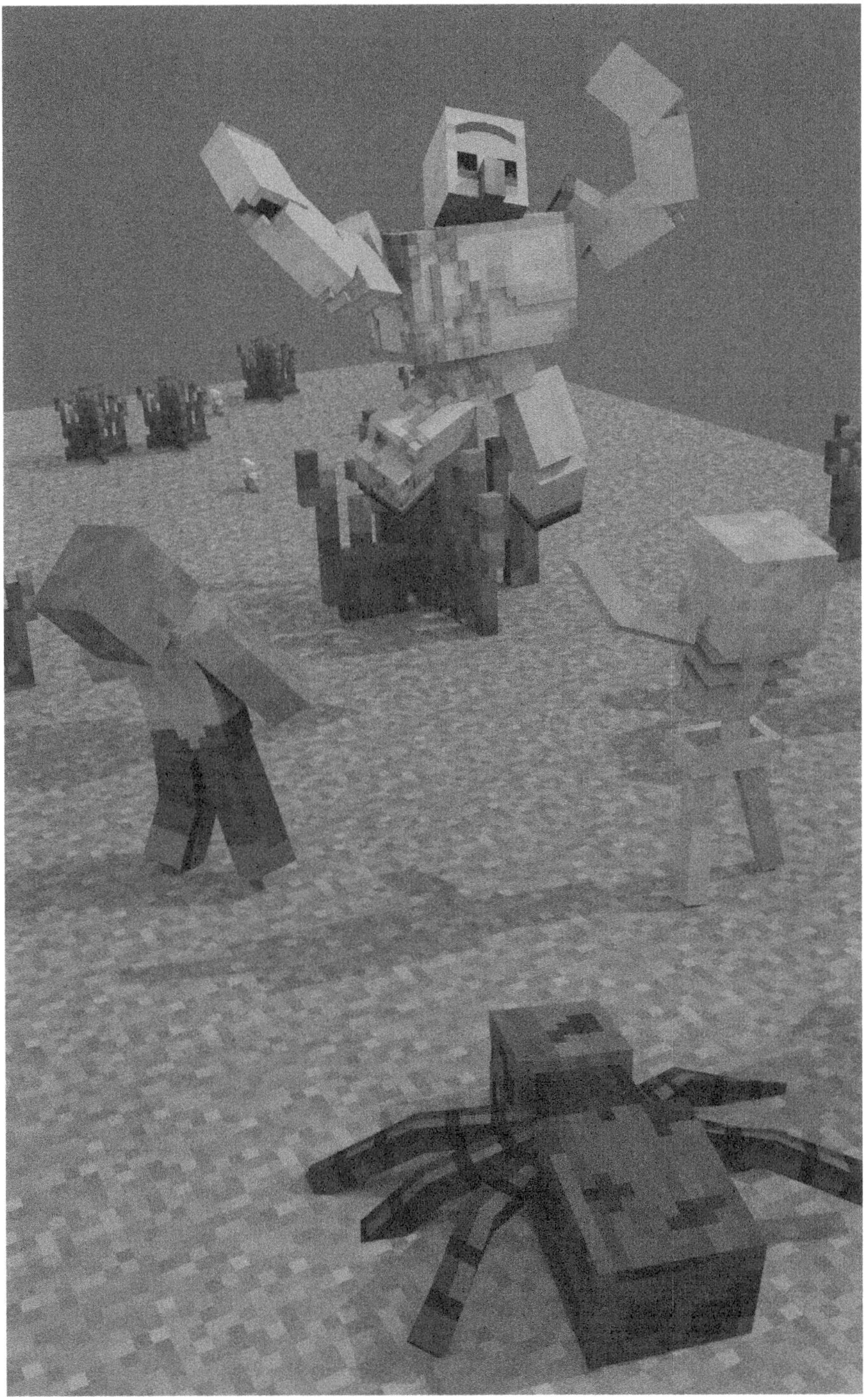

Can You Help Me Out?

Thanks for reading all the way through. I hope that you enjoyed this book. As a new writer, it is hard to get started; it is difficult to find an audience that wants to read my books. There are millions of books out there and sometimes it is super hard to find one specific book. But that's where you come in! You can help other readers find my books by leaving a simple review. It doesn't have to be a lengthy or well written review; it just has to be a few words and then click on the stars. It would take less than 5 minutes.

Seriously, that would help me so much, you don't even realize it. Every time I get a review, good or bad, it just fills me with motivation to keep on writing. It is a great feeling to know that somewhere out there, there are people who actually enjoy reading my books. Anyway, I would super appreciate it, thanks.

If you see new books from me in the future, you will know that I wrote them because of your support. Thank you for supporting my work.

Special thanks again to previous readers and reviewers. Thank you for encouraging me to keep writing. I'll do my best to provide high quality books for you all.

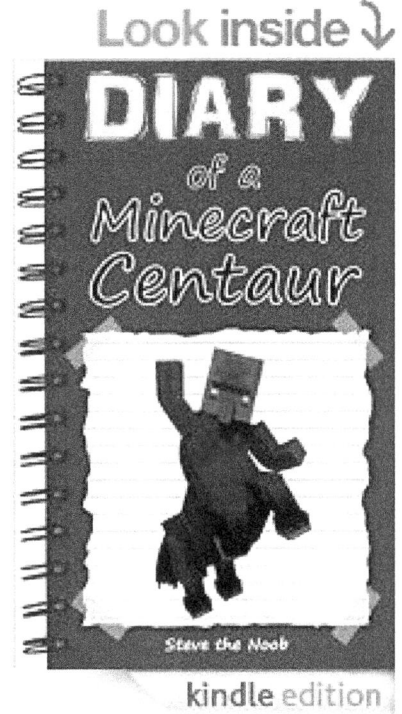

My Other Books

Check Out My Author Page
Steve the Noob

My Awesome List of Favorite Readers and Reviewers

My Awesome List of Favorite Readers and Reviewers

W. shi "Jenn"

K.K "mysweetdees"

Mikail

WarCenturion

Stephanie Linn

Thank you so much for your support. You guys and girls rock!!

- Jewel Shine
- Minoscreeperslayer
- RainbowCreeper
- Sang Chul Choi
- Misahti
- Panisara W.
- Astro Cat
- AthanEnder
- betsy
- akaherobrine
- James
- Xaxier Edwards
- leann xiao
- Awesomeguy27

Made in the USA
Las Vegas, NV
30 January 2021